INVEST

in the

BEST

Other books in the *Wiley Investment* series:

Angel Financing: How to Find and Invest in Private Equity
Gerald A. Benjamin & Joel Margulis
Cyber-Investing: Cracking Wall Street with Your PC, 2nd Ed. David L. Brown & Kassandra Bentley
Lessons from the Front Line: Market Tools and Investing Tactics from the Pros
Michael Brush
The Money Flood: How Pension Funds Revolutionized Investing
Michael J. Clowes
The Investor's Anthology: Original Ideas from the Industry's Greatest Minds
Charles Ellis with James R. Vertin
Mutual Funds on the Net: Making Money Online Paul B. Farrell
It Was a Very Good Year: Extraordinary Moments in Stock Market History
Martin S. Fridson
Invest in the Best: How to Profit from Well-Managed Companies Stephen George
The Conservative Investor's Guide to Trading Options LeRoy Gross
Stock Investing for Everyone: Tools for Investing Like the Pros Arshad Khan & Vaqar Zubei
Puzzles of Finance: Six Practical Problems and Their Remarkable Solutions
Mark Kritzman
The Psychology of Investing Lawrence E. Lifson & Richard Geist
Merton Miller on Derivatives Merton Miller
REITs: Building Your Profits with Real Estate Investment Trusts John Mullaney
The Inner Game of Investing: Access the Power of Your Investment Personality
Derrick Niederman
Patterns in the Dark: Understanding Risk and Financial Crisis with Complexity Theory Edgar E. Peters
The Art of Short Selling Kathryn F. Staley
The Stock Market, 7th Ed. Richard J. Teweles & Edward S. Bradley
Searching for Alpha: The Quest for Exceptional Investment Performance
Ben Warwick
Market Magic: Riding the Greatest Bull Market of the Century Louise Yamada

Forthcoming:
Promoting Prosperity: The Growth and Implications of Global Wealth
John Edmunds
The Prudent Investor's Guide to Hedge Funds: Profiting from Uncertainty and Volatility James P. Owen

INVEST *in the* BEST

How to Profit from Well-Managed Companies

Stephen George

John Wiley & Sons, Inc.
New York • Chichester • Weinheim • Brisbane • Singapore • Toronto

This book is printed on acid-free paper. ∞

Published by John Wiley & Sons, Inc.

Published simultaneously in Canada.

Library of Congress Cataloging-in-Publication Data:
George, Stephen, 1948–
Invest in the best : how to profit from well-managed companies / Stephen George.
p. cm.—(Wiley investment series)
ISBN 0-471-38510-7 (cloth : alk. paper)
1. Investment analysis. 2. Corporations—Evaluation. 3. Management—Evaluation. 4. Investments. I. Title. II. Series.
HG4529 .G46 2000
332.6—dc21 00-033004

Printed in the United States of America

10 9 8 7 6 5 4 3 2 1

Contents

Preface

No matter what theory of investing you hold, regardless of the strategy or discipline you follow, your approach carries some degree of risk. I think investing in well-managed companies helps you reduce that risk. Even better, it can improve the return on your investments. Better yet, it works with nearly every investment approach.

Why invest in well-managed companies? Their customers love them. Their employees swear by them. They boast superior quality, innovative products and services, efficient processes, and visionary leadership. Best of all, at least for investors, *they deliver profits.* There's been some doubt about that, some questions about whether quality of management has any measurable effect on the bottom line. It does, and I'll prove it. Investing in well-managed companies turns out to be a sound investment strategy.

None of which means you should stop evaluating their financial performance. If you dote on price-to-earnings (P/E) ratios, market capitalization, projected revenues, and other financial indicators, feel free to continue doting. There are a lot of books and Web sites out there that can advise you on what these indicators mean and how you can analyze them. This book supports them. The truth is, you don't need another author telling you how to interpret the same financial information everyone has, but you do need an author who can tell you how to interpret the quality of a company's management using information few people have—and even fewer understand. Such rare knowledge may be just the edge you need to beat the average.

The ability to identify well-managed companies can give you

greater confidence in your investments. As I will demonstrate, being well-managed is a leading indicator of earnings and P/E ratio success.

The first thing you need to understand is what makes a well-managed company. Why do their customers love them? Why do their employees love them? How can they deliver quality and innovation faster than their competitors and still increase revenues and reduce costs? And what does all this mean to investors? I've worked with more than a dozen terrific companies in the past decade and researched and written about a hundred more. I'll tell you what a well-managed company looks like and the signs you can spot that will help you track them down.

Let's say you already have a potential investment in your sights. Maybe it's a hot tip your brother-in-law passed along. Maybe it's a local company you've been reading about. Maybe it's an up-and-comer eating your company's lunch. You gather the numbers and do your financial analysis but the data paint an incomplete picture. A company is people, yet people have no place in the financial equation. You need to know more about the people producing the numbers. You need to evaluate the quality of this potential investment's management. You turn to the Management Screen.

I created the Management Screen to give investors a tool for assessing the quality of a company's management system. Just don't confuse this process or the results with the financial analysis you conduct. The two kinds of information could not be more different. Management information doesn't reside in one place. None of it exists in a standardized format. The evaluation never depends on universal numbers, such as a P/E ratio, and rarely is it a simple, apples-to-apples comparison. You won't find a zillion Web sites offering complete management information and a host of ways to slice it, as you can with financial information.

The benefit of studying a potential investment's *financial* situation is that consistent, reliable, timely data are readily available to all investors. The drawback to this approach is that the data and analysis are available to all investors. Everyone crunches the same numbers, including some very smart, well-informed experts. Where's the advantage in that?

The problem with studying a potential investment's *management* quality is that consistent, reliable, timely data are hard to find. That's also your greatest advantage. I'll tell you how to dig for data that illuminate the quality of a company's management system. I'll point you to sources you can tap into for tips about companies on the quality journey. And I'll tell you what to do with what you find.

The point of this book is not to applaud well-managed companies, although they deserve all the accolades they get. No; the point of this book is to help you profit by investing in these companies. To do that, you need to know what well-managed companies look like, how you can find them, how you can evaluate any company's management, and how you use the Management Screen to further refine your investment strategies.

You also need to believe that management has an impact on a company's stock price. That's where the Quality Index comes in. If you take the 100 best-managed companies out of the Standard & Poor's 500, maintaining the same diversity and weighting, guess what? Those 100 returned 26% in 1999 compared to 21% for the S&P 500. I've mind-melded with the creators of the Quality Index (at least that's what it felt like) and I'll explain how they built it and what it means.

No investor wants to leave money on the table. All things being equal except the quality of management, you're likely to earn more if you factor quality of management into your investment decisions. *Invest in the Best* explains why, and it explains how you can do it. All you need is the desire to root out—and profit from—well-managed companies.

Acknowledgments

Craig Robinson and Mark Billeadeau inspired this book with their innovative Q-100, which, I hope, will help inspire even more companies to pursue quality management. They're two quality guys and I thank them for all their help.

Speaking of quality guys, Gary Floss and Arnie Weimerskirch, both past leaders of the Baldrige Panel of Judges, were gracious enough to read the manuscript and help make it better. Thanks, Gary and Arnie.

I also want to thank my family for putting up with me while I wrestled with this book. Zack, Allie, Katie, Dan, Ben, and Ellen—thanks!

INVEST
in the
BEST

Chapter 1

What's Missing in Your Stock Analysis

Boy, it's hard to find an advantage in the stock market these days. I mean, anybody can access and analyze the same financial information about publicly traded companies. Log onto the Internet and in no time an investor can find out what business a company's in, its current and historical financial performance, how it compares to the rest of its industry, what its projected earnings are, and whether experts think its stock should be bought, held, or sold.

If that's not enough, you can spend a few bucks to get "inside" information from stockbrokers and analysts who filter the same financial data through a deeper understanding of a particular company, industry, or sector. Their recommendations wander from the fundamental or technical analysis of financial performance to the grayer areas of trends and possibilities. Rumored mergers and acquisitions trigger such advice. New technologies and innovative products set them off. On the Internet side, a perceived competitive advantage quickly runs up the stock price.

Of course, none of this analysis, including the financial analysis, is a black-and-white proposition. Two investors can look at the same price-to-earnings ratios and arrive at completely different conclusions, just as two investors can learn about an Internet stock's potential and take opposite positions. It's all open to interpretation. With that in mind, how would you have interpreted the potential of a company called Solectron (SLR), which provides manufacturing services to electronics equipment manufacturers?

Let me give you a little background. Founded in 1977, Solectron began as a small job shop in Milpitas, California. To make money on the razor-thin margins common in the electronics industry, Solectron quickly realized it had no room for error. It had to build flawless products at a competitive price, and it had to deliver them on time. Like most electronics companies, it turned to *total quality management* (a dynamic science that includes Six Sigma) as a means of improving quality, cutting costs, building profits, and growing the business.

The strategy worked. Solectron grew throughout the 1980s, earning 27 superior performance awards from its customers. By 1991 it had more than 2,000 employees at five sites in and around Milpitas, yet it was still just one of many printed circuitboard manufacturers. Its price-to-earnings ratio stood at 13 at the start of that year, with earnings per share of a penny. Industry analysts liked the company's potential, but few outside that small world even realized Solectron existed. How would you have assessed its position?

How about some more information—understanding that it's not the type of information most investors think is worthwhile? In 1990 Solectron became a finalist for the Malcolm Baldrige National Quality Award. It didn't win that year, but it did in 1991, the same year it committed to surpassing Six Sigma quality in its critical processes by 1996. (I'll explain Six Sigma and its relevance in Chapter 4.) It determined customer satisfaction *weekly*, a frequency that's still rare in the business world today. It trained and empowered its multilingual workforce, composed of people from 20 cultures.

Blah, blah; I know. Be patient. You may be thinking this is already more than you wanted to know about the company, but stick with me here. You won't want to miss the punch line.

Imagine it's 1991 and your investment strategy is to *invest in the best.* You're a forward-thinking investor and you've come up with criteria for deciding what "the best" are. Solectron pops up on your radar because of the supplier awards and Baldrige thing. You screen it using your criteria and, *voila*! Solectron qualifies, easily. So you put $1,000 into Solectron stock, then sit back and watch.

The company grows quickly. By 1997 it has added 16,000 employees and 17 sites around the world. Quality and customer loyalty remain high. Its market share has doubled as its stock outpaces the Standard & Poor's 500.

Solectron wins its second Baldrige Award in 1997, confirming its status as one of the world's best-managed companies and reassuring you that your investment is sound. Only now, more investors are jumping on the bandwagon, not because of Solectron's managerial competence, but because of its strong financial performance.

You hang onto your stock. By 1999 Solectron is the world's largest electronics contract manufacturer and the tenth-largest company in Silicon Valley. At the end of 1999, you calculate the return on your original investment and discover, to your delight, that you have, indeed, profited from this well-managed company (see Figure 1.1).

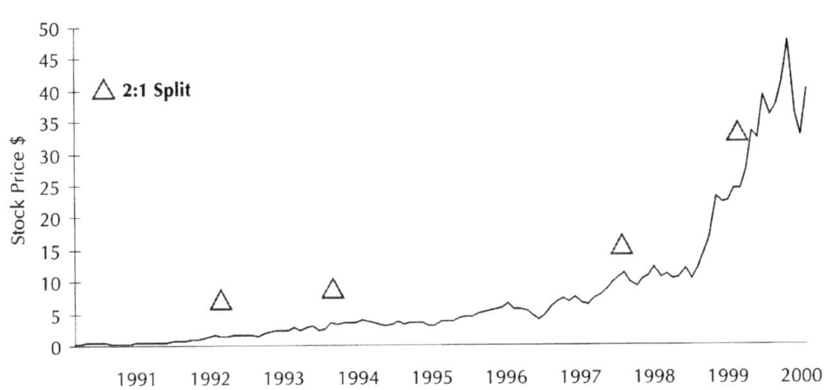

Figure 1.1 Solectron Corporation's Stock Performance

The stock you paid $1,000 for eight years earlier is now worth nearly $130,000!

Finding the Next Solectron

Okay, I admit that's an extremely positive example. We all know about the rare stock that delivers extraordinary returns *if* you invest in it at the right time. And that's the point of the story, not to hammer you with another missed opportunity, but to lure you into considering the tremendous upside of factoring management quality into your investment decisions. I mean, let's face it, if you were buying stocks in 1991, would Solectron, the company or the stock, have even crossed your mind? If you're investing today and you honestly weigh the information I just provided, would Solectron make your list of possible investments?

What if you could have invested in an index fund in 1999 that included 100 companies from the Standard & Poor's 500 that covered the same sectors as the S&P 500 but that returned 22% more than an S&P 500 index fund? I'll explain what that 100-company fund is in the next chapter, but the only distinction between those 100 companies and the rest of the S&P 500 was managerial competence. That 22% edge reflects the real value of quality management.

The purpose of this book is to help you find and profit from the Solectrons of the world before everybody else knows they're a good investment. But that's not its only purpose. In this book you'll learn:

- Why the stock of well-managed companies is a good investment (trust me, not everyone believes this matters)
- What makes a well-managed company
- How you can find well-managed companies
- How you can add a Management Screen to your stock analysis approach
- When to act on what you learn

I should also warn you about what you won't find in this book:

- Fundamental analysis or technical analysis or any related approaches to evaluating or choosing stocks based solely on their financial performance
- Debate about value versus growth
- Arguments for or against tech stocks
- Discussion about index funds versus mutual funds

Does the book talk about financial performance? Absolutely. Will it help you if you're a value investor or a growth investor or a tech stock aficionado? Definitely. And it will do this by giving you insights into management that aren't available from any other sources.

This isn't your typical investment book. But then, I'm not your typical investment book author. I know a whole lot more about managerial competence than I do about investment analysis, and I intend to stick to what I know. And what I know is that quality of management usually has a direct impact on how well a company performs—and that includes the performance of its stock.

I'm not saying that management is the deciding factor in a company's stock performance, or even that it's the most important factor. The best-managed company in the world can still fail for any number of reasons, including its industry taking a dive, unexpected regulatory or legal issues, mergers and acquisitions, changes in the economy, or changes in the market. Well-managed companies can weather these challenges better than their competitors and, in some cases, improve their position, but they cannot chug merrily along in their own narrow world. What they can do is make the best of their resources and opportunities so that the ups are stronger and longer and the downs aren't as deep or destructive. And that's why quality management is critical.

Yet if management is so important, why do brokers and analysts pretty much ignore it when they study a company's stock? I'll tell you why: Few have a proven process for evaluating it. In an article I recently read, one broker said, "With most companies I want to know two basic things: where it and its products are positioned within the industry, and how it intends to sell its products." While these concerns get at some of the responsibilities of management, they by no means address all the areas that determine the quality of a management system.

Another broker said his objective "is to know how these companies are doing as opposed to what they are doing." That's the typical financial bias speaking. A third broker said he was "definitely" interested in the quality of management, "but basically, we analyze the financial numbers." Being interested in management quality is a far cry from being able to assess it.

Fewer individual investment books have had greater success recently than those flying the Motley Fool banner. David and Tom Gardner strive to make investing accessible to anyone. In *The Motley Fool Investment Workbook*, they write, "Looking for great individual stocks to research and invest in is no more difficult than studying the companies that provide great products or services in your life." Their idea of studying companies, like that of most advisors, is to analyze the financial data, as if financial data alone can point you to great individual stocks.

Stockbrokers and analysts are loaded with financial information and they can analyze it a thousand different ways. The proliferation of investment gurus, such as the Gardner brothers, in print and on television attests to the hunger for sound stock market advice, but it also numbs readers and viewers with the sameness of it all. Nine times out of ten, an analyst's "hot tip" about a company's stock hinges on rumors that earnings will be higher or lower than projected, or that the company is buying—or being bought by—another, or that the landscape of the company's industry is changing.

These opinions rarely take into account the company's managerial competence—unless the senior leader botched the job. The inability to confidently assess managerial competence is a problem that has plagued investors and their advisors for decades.

Investing in a Fog

In Wall Street a great deal is constantly said [about management], but little that is really helpful. Until objective, quantitative, and reasonably reliable tests of managerial competence are devised and applied, this factor will continue to be looked at through a fog.

Benjamin Graham
The Intelligent Investor

Investors and potential investors know about the fog. Of all the investment advice in all the investment joints in all the world, nobody has been able to tell you how to assess managerial competence and lift the fog. Even Mr. Graham peered through that fog, and he wrote one of the definitive books on investing and served as a mentor to Warren Buffett.

Which doesn't mean that analysts, brokers, and fund managers just ignore management. It's just that they confuse the practice of management with the people who manage. Business magazines and newspapers fill column after column with stories about the people leading the companies whose stock is under scrutiny. It's the cult of personality—*People* magazine in the business arena. Buy Blunderbuss Inc. because the new CEO knows how to streamline a company. Sell Musket Scents because the CEO has lost his touch.

The most popular method of assessing managerial competence typically involves speculating on the abilities of senior leadership and, most often, *the* senior leader. When investment insiders believe a company is faltering, they question the competence of the chief executive. When they recommend buying a stock, they pin their hopes on the ability of the chief executive. Managerial competence becomes CEO competence, meaning the tests of that competence fall far short of Graham's criteria: objective, quantitative, and reasonably reliable.

Investors suffer the consequences. With little information about managerial competence at hand, we must assume that a competent leader means competent management. Few of us are willing to put our money where our assumptions are. Instead, we ignore the managerial competence issue completely. We figure the ratios and analyze the numbers and bet on value or growth or whatever combination we prefer. We study the charts of past performance and project future results and turn where the statistics tell us.

Open your favorite investment book and count the number of pages devoted to statistics: market capitalization . . . revenues . . . price-to-earnings (P/E) ratios . . . cash flow. Public companies provide financial information. Analysts, brokers, and fund managers analyze that information. The numbers present a relatively black-and-white case and they're defensible: Rank the stocks by earnings per share; identify the highest-yielding stocks; consider how rapidly earnings and revenues are growing; only buy reasonable P/E ratios; look for a healthy return on equity. In a business dependent on people parting with their hard-earned money, being able to defend your recommendations is a big deal. The language of financial performance allows brokers, analysts, and investors to explain why, to argue for or against, and to rationalize the losses. Better yet, they seem to eliminate the need to know anything about how a company is managed. If you trust the numbers and the analysis of them, you need not venture into that management quagmire.

This blind faith in the financials is misplaced. While the numbers tell you where a company has been, they have limited ability to tell you where it's going. It's like driving a bus while looking in the rearview mirror. Smart executives have learned they can't lead a company this way, but investors have had little choice when it comes to owning stock in a company. The financial information is readily available while management information is not. Financial information allows analysis and comparisons. Some would like to believe it permits prediction, but while past performance may suggest future results, it in no way assures them.

Behind the Numbers

Consider Dell Computer Corporation. If past financial results truly predicted future performance, investors would be snapping up all the

Dell stock they could afford—which, for most of the 1990s, is exactly what they've been doing (see Figure 1.2).

Dell is the fastest growing computer manufacturer in the world, surpassing all of its competitors in PC sales except Compaq in the global market, and it has Compaq in its sights. Relying on its highly effective "direct model," Dell eliminates the middle man and sells directly to companies and individuals. Competitors that must sell through distributors cannot compete on price, speed of delivery, or customization. As a result, Dell has been gobbling up market share at an astounding pace, and investors have reaped the rewards. At least until 1999.

In the fall of 1997, Dell hired me to help one of its manufacturing facilities apply for the Texas Quality Award (TQA). The facility is truly impressive. Trucks filled with computer parts back up to a row of bays on the west side of the building. The trucks serve as the facility's warehouse, providing just-in-time components for the day's production. A half-dozen manufacturing lines build computers to specific customer orders. Each configuration depends on a customer's choices. Each system has already been bought and, often, paid for. Components are collected, units as-

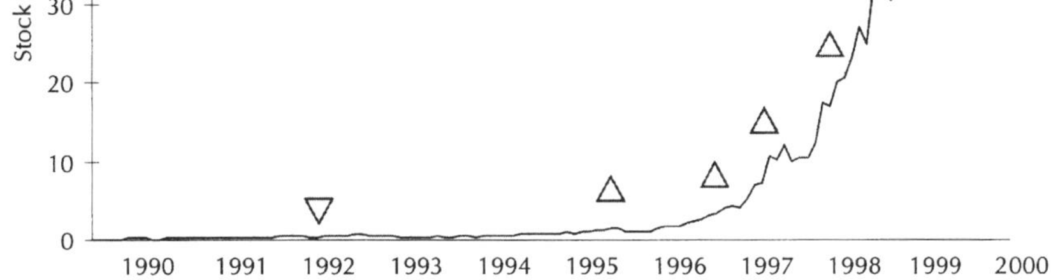

Figure 1.2 **Dell Computer Corporation's Stock Performance**

sembled and tested, and systems packaged and moved onto trucks on the east side of the facility. The entire process took less than four hours then—and I imagine it's gotten faster. Engineers constantly evaluate the steps and tasks in the manufacturing process to identify opportunities to improve quality and reduce cycle time. At any moment, one or two lines are being revamped to take advantage of what has been learned on the other lines and to pilot new approaches. Quality improvement teams form to tackle critical problems that are impeding performance.

It is a productive operation. When the TQA examiners studied it, they were mesmerized by the speed at which products were made and processes altered. Dell people call it "moving at Dell speed." Observing the construction of computers in a span of a few hours, considering the company's unbelievable string of consecutive quarters in which earnings were at least 50% greater than the previous quarter, it was impossible not to believe this is a world-class organization.

The Dell facility won the Texas Quality Award. To interested observers, the honor confirmed their belief that Dell is a well-managed company deserving their investment dollar. That conclusion, however, was misleading.

The first caveat came from the nature of the award. State quality awards struggle to attract attention. Many have expanded their potential customer base by adding awards for education, government, health care, and not-for-profit organizations. Many have gone to multilevel awards, extending recognition from quality newcomers all the way up to fairly mature quality programs. Their judging standards tend to be more generous than the national Baldrige Award, in part because they want to encourage organizations to participate. Honoring popular companies such as Dell brings statewide media attention to the program and valuable support from the winning company. While a state quality award winner must have sound, systematic quality improvement practices in place, its management system is usually not as mature as that of a Baldrige Award winner and, for that reason, contains more significant gaps that may hurt performance.

The second caution came from the winning organization itself. The facility that won the award is one of several Dell facilities manufacturing one of several product lines. Dell didn't win the award; a unit of Dell did. Assuming that an entire company is well-managed because one unit earns quality recognition can be a costly mistake.

As it turned out, Dell's phenomenal growth slowed in 1999. Its stock price, which Dell has long claimed is the best measure of its success, has been stagnant for the first time in nearly a decade.

I know this is a lot to throw at you right now—Baldrige and state awards, management processes—and I'll explain what they are and what they mean later. For now, I want to emphasize that past financial performance in no way predicts the future, and neither does management performance. Many of this country's foremost investment advisors depend on the tenuous practice of using past financial performance to predict future earnings and growth. But that doesn't mean they like it.

Warren Buffett once said, "When I buy a stock, I think of it in terms of buying a whole company, just as if I were buying the store down the street. If I were buying the store, I'd want to know all about it." His main source of material about a company is its annual report and the reports of its competitors. Analysts read annual reports because of the financial information they present, not for the hyperbole that accompanies it. If an investment analyst was interested in buying the store down the street, he or she would probably ask to see the books, then make a decision with little thought of managerial competence. For most investment advisors, "knowing all about a company" means knowing where it stands financially.

Peter Lynch recommends "kicking the tires." Visit one of the company's stores. Try out its products or services. He writes, "Investing without research is like playing stud poker and never looking at the cards." In his case, however, as in Buffett's case, the "cards" reveal only the financial condition of the company. Assessing the quality of its management depends on vague impressions gained by "kicking the tires."

Benjamin Graham has been called the greatest investment advisor of the twentieth century, but even he could find no reliable test of managerial competence. Despite his frustration, he still listed "management" as the second most important factor in evaluating common stock. (The first factor was a company's general long-term prospects.) And he longed for objective, quantitative, and reasonably reliable tests of managerial competence.

At last, a fresh breeze is blowing away the fog Graham first wrote about 50 years ago.

What Managerial Competence Means

To an investor, "managerial competence" means increasing the price of the company's shares. If the value of my shares grows, management is competent. If they lose value, management stinks!

The trick, of course, is figuring out whether the stock is going to gain or lose value. Anxious investors scan business publications for clues about where management might be taking the companies whose stock they own. For their part, the publications scrutinize management through the investor's lens, reacting to disappointing earnings by questioning a company's strategies concerning product or service innovation, marketing, competition, cost control, and other factors they believe shape the company's success.

Such analysis rarely lives up to Graham's criteria of objective, quantitative, or reasonably reliable. Investors and the publications they read must rely on what they know, and what they know are financial results. The tests of managerial competence remain outside their purview.

What does managerial competence mean? If you've worked for a company, you have some idea of what it is—and what it isn't. We'll nail this down in the next three chapters, but just so you know what I've been talking about, let's name the key qualities of a well-managed company.

The first quality has to be *visionary leadership*. Senior leaders need to set breakthrough expectations for the company and ensure the creation of strategies, systems, and methods that move the company in that direction. There's a reason business publications dote on business leaders: They define a company's culture and keep the company focused on what's important. The best possess a unique ability to articulate a shared vision that all employees can own and work toward.

What's important for every company is its customers. A company cannot increase earnings without gaining new customers and retaining loyal customers. Companies perform well when they are sensitive to their customers' changing requirements, aware of changes in technology and competition, and channeling their collective energy toward retaining customers and growing market share. For many world-class companies, this means bringing the key customers into the company and involving them in product and service design, strategic planning, and process improvement. The second quality of a well-managed company is a *focus on customers*.

The third quality of a well-managed company is *continuous improvement and learning*. The words "learning organization" have probably crossed your path in the last few years. "Knowledge management" is another popular phrase. Well-managed companies know how to capture and share knowledge and information to increase learning among all employees. They enhance value to customers through new and improved products and services. They identify and pounce on new business opportunities. They cut costs by reducing errors, defects, and waste. They make service a priority by shortening delivery times and improving responsiveness. They become more efficient by increasing productivity and the effective use of all resources. In the process, they gain an edge in the marketplace—and become more valuable to investors.

Well-managed companies accomplish this through the knowledge, skills, creativity, and motivation of their employees. A well-managed company *values its employees*. To increase revenues while reducing costs, today's companies must be fast, flexible, focused, and flat, characteristics identified by Rosabeth Moss Kanter in her book, *World Class*. A company cannot achieve this desirable state in a hierarchical, command-and-control structure. Being world class demands a high-performance workforce comprised of individuals trained and empowered to take initiative and responsibility.

Well-managed companies align the efforts of all employees through a dynamic strategic plan. The plan takes into account the needs of all stakeholders, including stockholders. It anticipates short- and long-term changes in such key areas as customer requirements, competition, industry, technology, the economy, and society. A *long-range view of the future* helps well-managed companies anticipate and take advantage of the changes that decimate less-prepared organizations.

They base their long-range view on critical data and information from a variety of sources including customers, suppliers, products and services, operations, employees, competitive comparisons, and finance. A well-managed company *manages by fact*. It collects and analyzes data and information to support planning, review performance, and improve operations. It gathers comparative information to understand exactly how well it is performing compared with key competitors and industry leaders. Unlike poorly managed companies, it can tell you exactly how the company is performing today and what those results mean for tomorrow.

This data-driven mentality allows the company to target those results that create and balance value for all stakeholders, including investors. A well-managed company *focuses on results*. Stockbrokers and analysts often question whether the company is focusing on the *right* results, an issue that usually surfaces when the long-term needs of the company don't jive with the short-term interests of some investors, but a well-managed company recognizes the need to increase current earnings without sacrificing future success. Such a common-sense approach may not satisfy those looking for a quick return on their money, but it should reassure investors who seek a more secure and profitable investment.

You can use the following qualities to assess managerial competence. I'll explain each in more detail in Chapters 3 and 4:

- Guided by effective leaders
- Focuses on customers

- Continuously improving
- Values employees
- Takes a long-range view of the future
- Manages by fact
- Demands results

Would you invest in a company that could demonstrate competence in all of these areas? Maybe; if you're like me, you'd still want to know what their competence has meant to the bottom line. After all, we don't buy stock in a company because we love its management but because we love what its management produces. But first, we need to buy into the argument that managerial competence directly affects stock performance, and that such competence can be determined.

Where Managerial Competence Resides

The first step in assessing managerial competence is to find companies with competent management. This used to be an insurmountable obstacle. Annual reports and other corporate communication fall far short of candid and complete when it comes to management. Even if you are able to meet with a company's executives, the biased and selective information you could glean does not enable you to assess managerial competence. As Graham wrote, the tests of managerial competence should be objective, quantitative, and reasonably reliable. Anything less and the evaluation might as well be ignored—which is why the issue of managerial competence has long remained foggy.

That is changing. True tests of managerial competence now exist, in fact, have existed for more than a decade. Those who pass these tests are recognized for the quality of their management and, as a result, become excellent investment candidates.

In the late 1980s, American business leaders responded to the need for "objective, quantitative, and reasonably reliable tests of managerial competence" by encouraging Congress to create the Malcolm Baldrige National Quality Award. The criteria for the award, improved annually for more than a decade now, define the characteristics of a well-managed company. Millions of copies of the criteria have been distributed. Forty-two states have launched awards based on the Baldrige model, as have more than two dozen countries. The Baldrige model has set the standard for quality management.

Using the model, it is now possible to define and assess managerial competence in an objective, quantitative, and reliable way. This was the *first obstacle* to considering management in investment decisions. The *second obstacle*, establishing the link between management and stock performance, proved more difficult to overcome. Most companies that won the Baldrige Award could point to stellar financial performance, but such results failed to provide conclusive proof that quality management had a direct impact on the bottom line.

What Managerial Competence Has to Do with Stock Performance

In 1998, two college professors, Kevin Hendricks and Vinod Singhal, completed a five-year study comparing the performance of more than 600 publicly traded companies that had won quality awards with companies in the same industries and of similar size that had not. Each award winner had a corresponding control firm. The winners had been recognized by one or more of about 140 different award givers, including supplier quality awards from such companies as Eastman Kodak, Ford, General Electric, 3M, and Texas Instruments; state quality awards; and/or the Baldrige Award or Shingo Prize. I'll tell you more about each of these award givers in Chapter 6.

The study analyzed several key performance measures including operating income, sales, total assets, employees, return on sales, and return on assets for all companies in the sample.

Hendricks and Singhal examined performance over two five-year periods: the *implementation period*, which started six years before the winners earned their first quality award and ended one year before they won, and the *post-implementation period*, which started one year before the winners won and ended four years after winning. The researchers assumed that the implementation of total quality management (TQM) actually made a difference in a company's financial performance about a year before it won its first award, since it takes award givers up to nine months to evaluate and certify the effectiveness of the implementation. Taking Solectron's case, its implementation period would have been from 1985 to 1989 and its post-implementation period from 1990 to 1994.

For the first five-year stretch, the implementation period, the researchers found no significant differences in performance between the award winners and the control group. These results led to two conclusions. First, neither group outperformed the other before TQM was factored in. Second, the cost of implementing TQM did not negatively affect the performance of the award-winning companies.

However, when it came to the post-implementation period, major differences appeared, with award winners significantly outperforming their rivals. Operating income, total assets, and sales grew more than twice as fast for winners during the post-implementation period as they did for the control group. While the stock price of the control companies grew 75% in that five-year period, the stock price of the award winners surged 119% (see Figure 1.3).

Award winners and controls were neck-and-neck at one point in this race before the winners pulled away. Why? Because the winners effectively implemented a systematic approach to improving management quality while the control group did not. During the implementation period and before the winners won anything, winners and controls were equals. Once managerial competence was in place, the winners leapt ahead of their counterparts.

In this study, winning quality awards served as a proxy for managerial competence. The criteria for the awards meet Graham's standard of "objective, quantitative, and reasonably reliable," although there's a lot of variation in the scope and depth of the different criteria. However, even with this variation, the award winners in the

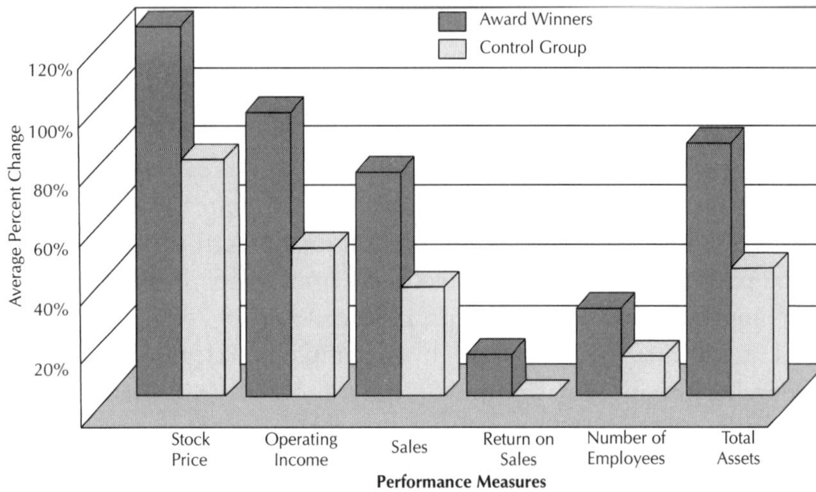

Figure 1.3 **Post-Implementation of TQM Comparison**
Source: Courtesy of Dr. Vinod Singhal and Dr. Kevin Hendricks

Hendricks/Singhal study smoked the competition. The study proved what investment experts and quality leaders have long believed: A *company that continuously improves the quality of its management system will perform better than a company that does not.*

Other studies support this conclusion. A 1992 study of more than 280 automotive suppliers found that they reported an average 17% increase in profits over a two- to three-year period due to continuous improvement efforts. A study by IBM in 1993 compared the performance of business units that scored 500 or more points on internal Baldrige assessments with business units that didn't reach that threshold. The business units that scored higher outperformed their counterparts in profitability, revenues, market share, employee morale, and customer satisfaction.

A recent study in Australia produced similar results. In February 1999, Alexander Hausner at the University of Wollongong released an independent study that found a strong correlation between performance in the Australian Quality Awards—a program based on the Baldrige model—and improvements in bottom line results. Paul

Clitheroe, director of IPAC Securities and host of the *Money* program on Sydney television, wrote in the *Sydney Morning Herald* that individual investors need to pay as much attention to the quality of management of companies they invest in as do professional fund managers and brokering analysts. "One way you can control risk is to avoid a company with poor quality management," said Clitheroe. "[Decent research] has an important role to play in removing the one risk that is quantifiable—the risk of your company being run by complete idiots."

Why Well-Managed Companies Are Undervalued

This brings us to the *third obstacle* to considering management in investment decisions: the missing link between the quality of management and the value of a company's stock. It is reasonable to assume that, when a company outperforms its competitors through quality management, its stock will have more value to investors. This hasn't been the case, however, *because the market systematically undervalues the effects of quality management*, usually until the financial payoff of quality management finally attracts investment dollars. Stockbrokers and analysts, unsure of managerial competence, give it almost no consideration when valuing stocks. If, as Hendricks and Singhal concluded, quality management improves a company's financial performance, including its stock performance, and if brokers and analysts don't account for this improvement in their recommendations, the stock of well-managed companies is consistently undervalued. *Investors who recognize this undervaluation before the rest of the investment community catches on have a distinctive advantage over their peers.*

How much of an advantage? You've seen the difference in stock performance in the study between award winners and the control group. *Based on these results, if you had invested in the study's 600 companies solely because they had implemented TQM, without giving any thought to what the financials were, you would have earned 58% more on your investment than if you'd put your money in the control group.*

Look again at the qualities of well-managed companies. The reason they outperform their competitors and provide value to investors is their sound, systematic approach to managing and improving all elements of their organizations. Well-managed companies anticipate and prepare for change. They make decisions based on current, relevant data and information. They use their planning processes and measurement systems to align the efforts of all employees with the companies' vision and objectives. They understand their core processes and constantly improve them. They know who their customers are and what they require and focus the entire organization on meeting those requirements.

While less-stellar companies bounce from one initiative to another, from one crisis to another, from peak to valley to plateau, well-managed companies take control of those elements that contribute to financial success. As a result, they are better able to respond to unexpected problems and opportunities. Their managerial competence lessens the risks associated with changes in the company, the industry, and the economy—and that makes well-managed companies an attractive investment.

Unfortunately, the beauty of these well-managed companies escapes most investors. As a result, the market systematically undervalues them. Hendricks and Singhal discovered that it can take two years after winning a quality award before a company begins to see the benefits of TQM on its stock price. While this span will surely shrink as more and more investors buy stock in award winners, it's still a window of opportunity you can use to your advantage.

An Index of Well-Managed Companies

One would think such compelling studies and conclusions would attract the attention of the big investment firms, and one would be correct. A few years ago, Fidelity Investments attempted to assess managerial competence by looking at those companies that had won the Baldrige Award and related state awards. They concluded that the list of winners was too short, the window of opportunity to invest before stock values rose too narrow, and the method of evaluating management too difficult to apply to a broader base of companies that hadn't won an award. They gave up.

About the same time, Robinson Capital Management, a small Midwestern money management firm, began developing their own index of well-managed companies. Robinson Capital Management manages General Securities, Inc., a mutual fund that the American Association of Individual Investors (AAII) consistently ranks among the top-performing flexible funds. More than two decades ago the founder of the fund, John P. "Jack" Robinson, concluded that companies serious about quality outperformed competitors that were not. While General Securities, Inc. applies a highly disciplined approach to evaluating companies on the basis of financial indicators, it also assesses companies' commitment to total quality management and continuous process improvement. Robinson Capital Management's expertise in developing and using this quality management screen sets it apart from other fund managers. It also provides the foundation for creating the first index that assesses and values well-managed companies: the Q-100.

I'll explain how Craig Robinson and Mark Billeadeau created the Q-100 in the next chapter. It's an intriguing story of innovation, persistence, and a firm belief in the value of quality management. The Q-100 takes advantage of the investment community's undervaluation of well-managed companies. By screening the Standard & Poor's 500 companies according to quality standards they developed, Robinson and Billeadeau identified a sector-neutral subset of 100 well-managed companies and put them in an index that they called the Q-100. In 1999, the S&P 500 earned a total return of 21.04%. The Q-100 earned 25.62%.

If you had invested in the Q-100 in 1999, you would have earned 22% more in a year than if you had invested in an S&P 500 index fund. And the primary reason for your good fortune would have been the value the Q-100 places on managerial competence. Ben Graham knew intuitively that "good managements produce a good average market price," as he wrote in *The Intelligent Investor*. Jack Robinson believed that total quality management affected stock price. The Q-100 proves that they were both right.

When to Buy Stock in Well-Managed Companies

What makes well-managed companies attractive *short-term* investments is the immediate impact on their financial performance when they begin to systematically improve management quality. As the Hendricks/Singhal study showed, well-managed companies begin to separate themselves from their competitors when their management systems are good enough to receive independent recognition. If you decide you want to invest in well-managed companies, you can buy their stock when such recognition is announced. The Appendix provides contact information for organizations that recognize managerial competence.

But you may not want to wait. As more and more investors apply some type of management screen to the companies they are considering, we can expect the value of well-managed companies to grow. Institutional investors have already shown interest in the Quality Index. At some point in the near future, the best time to buy will not be when awards are announced because those awards will recognize good financial results. The big institutions will be buying the same stock at the same time. The best time to buy will be when companies are in the early stages of improving their manage-rial competence. In most cases, this will be two or three years before they are good enough to win an award. If you can identify these companies before the quality of their management becomes public knowledge, you will be in position to profit from the short-term boost when they win an award and the long-term potential of a well-managed company.

Make no mistake, this is not a slam-dunk effort. Identifying companies on the road to managerial competence *before* they appear on most investors' radar requires a little research, an awareness of the signs of managerial competence, and the ability to distinguish between the devoted and the dilettante. Chapters 6 and 7 offer advice on how to identify well-managed companies, and Chapter 8 tells you how to factor managerial competence into your buying—and selling—decisions.

As Benjamin Graham wrote, management is a key factor in evaluating stock. But it's not the only factor. Financial performance, long-term prospects, financial strength, the industry, and the economy all contribute to an intelligent investment. Now, for the first time, you need not invest in a company sight unseen. With a little knowledge and research, you can be confident that the managerial competence of the companies you own will continue to make them profitable performers.

Chapter 2

Why Well-Managed Companies Are Good Investments

To understand the logic of investing in well-managed companies, you need only trace the journey of Jack Robinson. Jack could be the patron saint of a relatively small group of people who, with a few exceptions, are not well known: the leaders of well-managed companies. We know about a few of these people: Jack Welch at General Electric; maybe Herb Kelleher at Southwest Airlines. You can probably think of others, but for the most part, they're largely ignored because their companies' managerial competence is largely ignored.

Jack Robinson appreciated a well-managed company. He liked them so much he spent most of his life looking for them. Once he found a well-managed company that fit his value profile, he worked it into his mutual fund.

Jack jumped into the investment business the year after World War II ended, founding Craig-Hallum, Inc., a small investment banking/brokerage firm. In 1951 he launched a mutual fund called General Securities, Incorporated. Through four-plus decades of good times and bad, his mutual fund paid dividends, running up a streak of 188 consecutive quarterly dividends by the time Jack died in 1998.

Jack intuitively knew that investing in quality companies was a good idea, but he never had the resources to prove his case in any scientific way. He noticed that well-managed companies didn't get hit as hard when the market turned south, and they recovered quicker when the market improved. As his reputation grew, he was invited to serve on the boards of some of the quality companies he admired. One such stint opened his eyes to the power of a formal process for quality management.

Jack's perception of the business landscape shifted in the late 1970s while serving on the board of directors of an electrical component manufacturer. One of the company's major customers, Ford Motor Company, advised it at that time that it would not remain a Ford supplier unless it implemented total quality management (TQM).

While it turned its attention to TQM, Jack thought about the ramifications for the company and its competitors. If management quality becomes a competitive advantage, he realized, then well-managed companies should be able to increase their revenues and cut their costs, making them more profitable. Since buying a share of stock means you're buying a share of that company's profits or earning power, a company with the potential for greater profits or earning power seemed like a better investment. Jack had always been looking for a way to evaluate management at the companies whose stock he was considering. TQM represented the high bar of managerial competence. If a company made it over that bar, doors opened at great companies like Ford and Motorola. If these companies were using TQM to evaluate management, he concluded, then TQM was good enough for him.

He began learning about TQM and questioning the quality commitment and approaches of the companies that crossed his path. As his knowledge grew, he found himself using quality of management to distinguish between companies of relatively equal financial performance.

In 1988, Susan Peterson, Jack's daughter, told him that if this was what he believed, he owed it to General Securities' shareholders to tell them how he was screening management in his investment decisions. He agreed, putting his thoughts into General Securities' 1988 annual report:

> A new element has been added to the process of analyzing the investment outlook for companies. It is Total Quality Management using the principle outlined by Deming, Juran and Crosby.
>
> It is my belief that companies using the Deming philosophy of management will outperform companies not using these methods.
>
> Total Quality Management will become the dominant factor in our country's economic future in the next decade. Total Quality Management leads to higher quality and lower costs. It systematically reduces waste and inefficiency. It sets up the mechanism for bringing into the management circle . . . the workers on the line.
>
> Those companies that recognize and understand that it is a gradual and continuous process, will prosper. Those who do not may not be around in the next 5 to 10 years.
>
> Total Quality Management is the new factor in future growth. Growth will not just mean new products or new industries. Growth will mean companies using Total Quality Management, whether they are mature or emerging companies, manufacturing or service companies.

He put his mutual fund money where his mouth was, holding stock in Merck, Hewlett-Packard, Xerox, Johnson & Johnson, Eastman Kodak, and McDonald's, among others. While he used TQM and continuous process improvement to screen potential investments, the management screen came *after* a financial analysis of price-to-earnings ratios, growth rates, financial strength, dividend yields, and other factors. He bought value, not growth, which limited the possibilities to a lot of chemical and electronics companies. When these industries did well, the fund did well. When they struggled, so did the fund.

Finding Quality Companies

The effort to expand the pool of possibilities and develop a more systematic way of evaluating them started when Mark Billeadeau began working with Jack in 1993 and continued when he joined Jack at his new firm, Robinson Capital Management, the current investment advisor for General Securities, Inc. Mark is a walking database, knowledgeable about any number of industries and the nuances of how they work and who's supplying whom with what. His unbounded curiosity extends to field trips with his son to such local industries as a steel mill, where Mark asks how things work while his son marvels at the furnaces and hot steel. Pyrotechnics aside, Mark wants to know what materials the mill must buy and who supplies them. When he learns about a single product costing thousands of dollars apiece, a product the mill burns up at the rate of more than one a day, a product in a market dominated by one supplier, a smile crosses his face. He's found a possible investment worth further investigation.

He brings the same relentless pursuit of information to his work. Confronted with Jack's intuitive, value-driven approach to investing, Mark suggested a more systematic approach that might uncover opportunities beyond the fund's limited industry bias. Jack balked. He liked to know the companies well and buy them when they were undervalued, which was why General Securities owned stock in only 20 companies. He couldn't keep track of a bigger list.

Mark decided to seek a more systematic approach on his own, starting with identifying quality companies. "In 1995 we didn't have a good estimate of how many quality-oriented companies there were or know how to identify them," Mark said. "I figured the best place to start was to get all the quality award winners—Baldrige, state, Shingo—just to see how many there were."

He built on that list by adding companies whose leaders stated, through either executive interviews or newspaper or magazine articles, that they were involved in quality. He didn't try to compare companies, assess their degree of total quality management, or assign any scores. If they showed up on this rudimentary screen, they made the list.

To test whether quality companies outperformed their competitors, Mark made hypothetical investments in the companies on his list. They blew the S&P 500 away, but it wasn't a fair fight since Mark's list included several small companies. He needed a more reliable comparison.

Craig Robinson joined his father's company in early 1996. He brought with him a degree in Fine Arts, a penchant for marketing, and an equally strong belief in the value of TQM, serving on the board of directors of the Minnesota Council for Quality. Mark Bil????leadeau had an ally.

They approached Jack with an idea. Mark said, "How about if I create a quality-based stock index and we'll track the performance of our fund relative to the index so at board meetings, if our fund stinks and the index stinks, we can say with a certain amount of confidence, 'Look, the fish in the lake we fish in ain't biting. The quality pool isn't doing well.' Or, if quality companies are hot, that's why we're hot."

Jack wasn't swayed. After all, if the fund struggled he simply told his board that the companies it owned were struggling and that was good enough. Their trust in Jack's investment abilities, supported by his consistent track record, gave them complete faith in his management. Since Jack didn't need any more justification for his decisions, he thought the index idea was a waste of time. General Securities should stick to its knitting, which was value investing with a quality twist.

Mark's early results suggested that the focus of this strategy was misplaced. "The hard thing was talking to a guy who's been successfully managing a portfolio since God was a kid and telling him that the quality idea works, that you were right to latch on to quality, but that almost nothing else does," said Mark. "I didn't know how to tell him that."

So he didn't. Instead, he and Craig began searching for more definitive proof of the value of quality management, beginning with the creation of a quality index that could be fairly compared to the S&P 500. "I thought the way to do this was take a subset of the S&P and, to the extent possible, keep the industries and sectors neutral to the S&P so that this is just a quality bet, not a large cap bet or a small cap bet, financials or cyclicals or anything else," said Mark.

"Yet the list of quality award winners was too limited, so we had to develop quality indicators."

Since Jack had expressly told them not to bother, they worked on it at night, plotting their strategies in what they now refer to as their "night crossings."

Defining Quality Management

To create a quality subset of the S&P 500, Mark and Craig knew they must first find a more consistent and reliable way to identify quality companies. They started with the criteria for the Malcolm Baldrige National Quality Award.

The U.S. Congress legislated the Baldrige Award in 1987 to strengthen U.S. competitiveness by helping companies understand and improve their performance. The criteria achieve this goal by defining the key values and attributes of a well-managed company. While the initial criteria focused heavily on manufacturing, quality leaders have continually refined them since 1988 to the point where the criteria are now relevant to nearly all types and sizes of organizations. No other business model has been as widely debated and used: Forty-two states and more than two dozen countries now have quality award programs based on the Baldrige model.

Mark and Craig knew that not every well-managed company won, or even applied for, quality awards. To find these companies, they needed to know what signs of quality management they should be looking for. The Baldrige criteria provided a way.

The criteria consist of seven categories: leadership, strategic planning, customer and market focus, information and analysis, human resource focus, process management, and business results. Since Mark and Craig didn't have access to a company's internal knowledge of performance in these areas, they needed to find public information about a company's quality credentials or, failing that, public proxies for performance in each category.

"We're looking for a quality management system," said Craig, "and we don't care what a company calls it. Since it's very hard to evaluate a quality management system in its entirety, we have to evaluate the pieces."

They found books that identified "America's best companies" or "most successful companies" or companies with the "best practices," and added the companies to their list. They looked for public proxies for each Baldrige category, such as giving a quality score in the "human resource focus" category to companies that appeared on *Fortune* magazine's "100 Best Companies to Work For," understanding that people could argue that making such a list didn't guarantee any formal approach to quality. They needed some way of separating companies displaying managerial competence in these seven areas from those that didn't, and a public list gave them a way.

Over the next couple years, Mark and Craig developed proxies for most areas within the seven categories and a way to score performance in each. I'll talk about the sources of such information in Chapter 5 and a method you can use to score companies on your own in Chapter 6. By the summer of 1998 they had assigned quality scores to 131 of the S&P 500. "Ideally you'd like to have every company scored," Mark said, "but we just couldn't do that." To test their list, they sent the names of all 500 companies in the S&P index to three General Securities board members who also happened to be experts in TQM. They asked the three directors to rate each of the 500 companies according to their understanding of its involvement in quality.

"We then compared their lists to our list and found a ninety-plus percent overlap in the companies identified as involved in quality," said Mark. "That told us we were on the right track."

They also wanted to make sure the list wouldn't offend anybody. "We didn't want anyone in the quality community looking at our list and thinking, 'These aren't quality companies,' " Mark said. "And we didn't want someone on the financial side saying, 'Nobody's going to invest in *that.*' We tried to make the list acceptable to both the quality and financial sides."

Feeling comfortable with their list, Mark created an index fund on his computer and called Craig into his office before trying it out. While they talked, Jack walked in and asked them what they were up to. Like kids caught with their hands in the cookie jar, they explained the development of a quality index and how they were ready to test it. With Jack watching, Mark finished loading the program and pressed the key that would compare the performance of their index with that of the S&P 500. They held their breath while the computer crunched the numbers, then sighed with relief when the quality index performed even better than Mark and Craig had expected.

Jack died suddenly a week later. With Craig now presiding over General Securities and Mark serving as chief investment officer, the role of the index changed from nice support for the unquestioned decisions Jack had made to essential justification for the untested decisions Craig and Mark would now face.

Comparing the Q-100 with the S&P 500

Over the next few months the new leaders of General Securities fine-tuned their index, narrowing the list to the top 100 companies, weighting them in the same way Standard & Poor's weights its companies, and diversifying the list to align it with the sectors in the S&P 500. They established guidelines for how they would manage the index and adjusted it according to their guidelines. When Standard & Poor's added Solectron to its index toward the end of 1998, Mark added Solectron to the quality index, now dubbed the Q-100.

They started tracking the performance of the Q-100 on September 30, 1998. Figure 2.1 shows how the Q-100 compared with the S&P 500 from that date to March 31, 2000. While the S&P gained 50% over that period, the Q-100 earned slightly over 61%! Using a measure of management quality as the primary factor, the 100 best-managed companies in the S&P 500 would have paid an investor 22% more over this 18-month period than he or she would have realized on an S&P 500 index fund.

In 1988, when Jack Robinson finally believed that management quality affected stock performance, he announced his intent

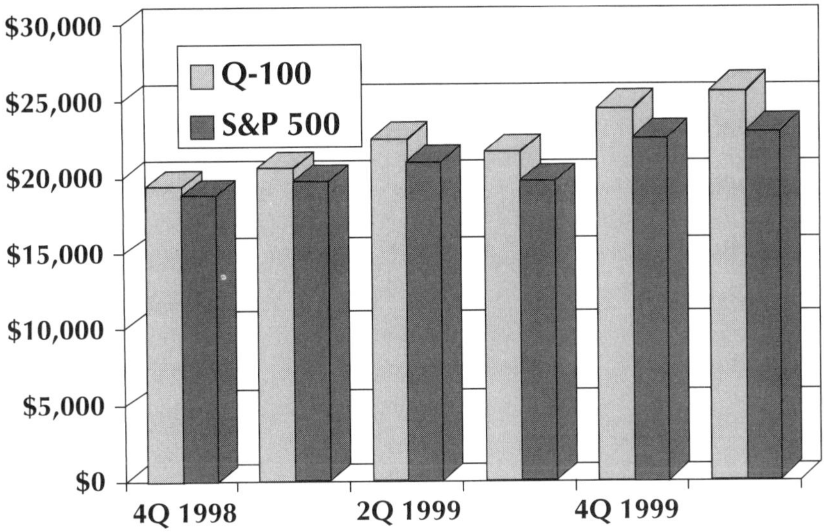

Figure 2.1 **Comparison of Q-100 and S&P 500 Performance**
Source: Robinson Capital Management

to use TQM and continuous process improvement as an additional analytic tool. In 1999, as the Q-100 racked up impressive results compared with the S&P and with the General Securities fund, Craig Robinson and Mark Billeadeau concluded that management quality should be their *primary* screening tool. They explored the possibility of converting General Securities, Inc. into an index fund using the Q-100, only to bump up against many of the fund's longstanding investment policies and guidelines typical of most investment companies. Intent on creating an investment strategy based on the Q-100 for the fund and other prospective investors, Mark and Craig went back three years and reweighted the companies in the Q-100. By applying a set of risk controls that further reduced the differences in economic sector and industry group weights between the Q-100 and the S&P 500, they created a truly "investable alternative" for quality-oriented investors (see Figures 2.2 and 2.3).

Fifty years ago, Benjamin Graham pleaded for "objective,

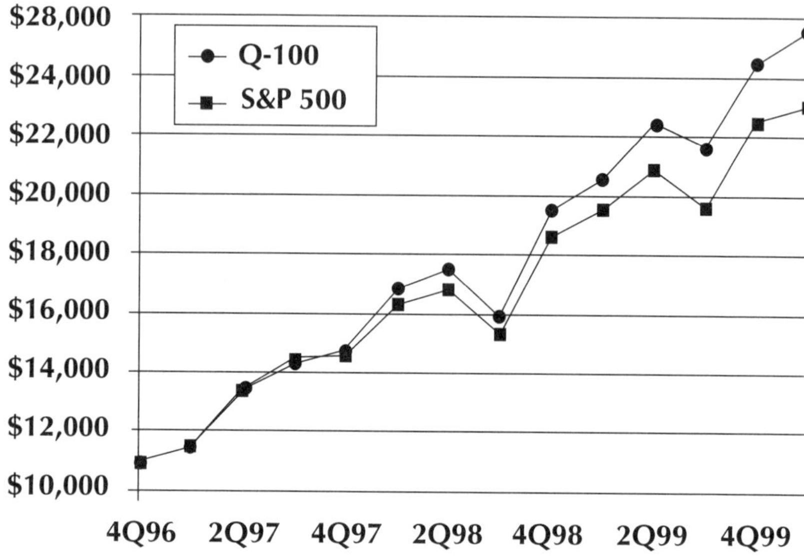

Figure 2.2 **Q-100 and S&P 500 Compounded Growth**
Source: Robinson Capital Management

quantitative, and reasonably reliable tests of managerial competence." We now have them.

When assembling the Q-100, Mark and Craig added a name to the list solely on the basis of outside recognition of that company's quality management system. They paged through books, scanned magazine articles, read executive interviews, and networked with quality leaders to find well-managed companies. To keep the list *objective*, they intentionally limited personal interaction with a possible candidate. "When companies are participating in quality improvement, they're cool places to be," said Craig. "We want to know what the outside world thinks of them. Otherwise, it's hard to establish relevance."

Both are aware that using outside sources in no way ensures that all well-managed companies can be identified. *Fortune* magazine's "Best Companies to Work For," for example, includes only compa-

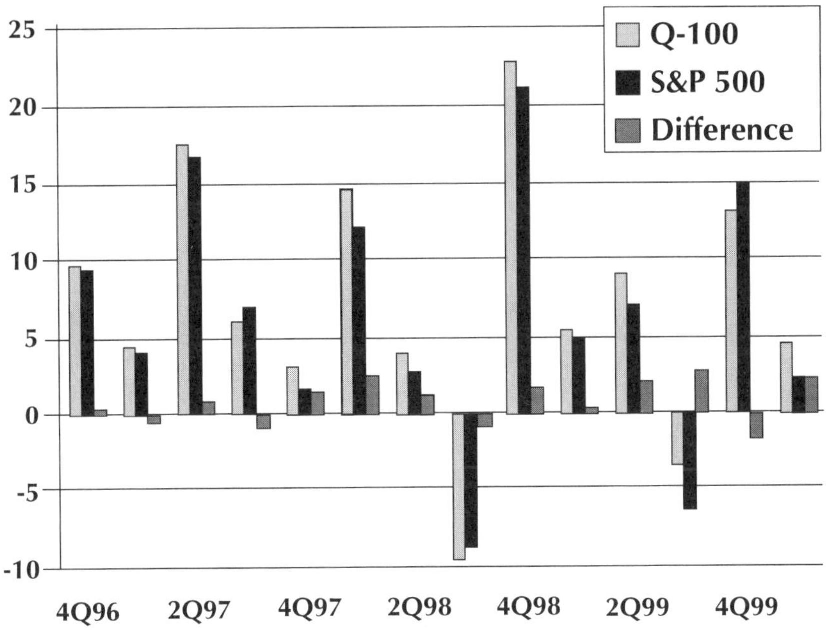

Figure 2.3 **Q-100 and S&P 500 Percent Change by Quarter**
Source: Robinson Capital Management

nies that nominated themselves for the honor. While *Fortune* surveys the entrants' employees to gauge their perceptions of their employers, companies that might be overflowing with happy employees never make the list because they don't apply. Mark and Craig try to fill this gap by including other sources of information about each element in a company's quality management system, but they acknowledge the flaws in this approach.

They also realize that their sources don't give them enough detailed information to allow them to rank companies according to the quality of their management systems. In the case of the best companies identified by *Fortune*, for example, they give every company on its list the same quality score. The companies may increase their scores by being recognized for quality in the same category or in any of the other six Baldrige categories. "All we can say with confidence is that *a* quality score is better than *no* quality score," said Mark.

Mark and Craig meet Graham's *quantitative* standard by: (1) using a comprehensive management model defined by the Baldrige criteria; and (2) identifying signals of excellent performance by companies in all or parts of the model. Many of the signals Mark and Craig found and still use are discussed in Chapter 5. The list stretches from the formal recognition bestowed by quality awards and quality system certification to the informal recognition produced by key word searches of business-related publications. As you will see, the results of such research, organized to cover the key elements of a management system, provide as quantitative a view of managerial competence as you're going to find without performing your own internal Baldrige assessment. Does it cover every element in a company's management system? Rarely; but as Mark and Craig have proven, it covers enough elements to produce a quantitative picture.

Graham also wrote that a test of managerial competence must be *reasonably reliable*. The study conducted by Kevin Hendricks and Vinod Singhal indicated that well-managed companies, identified by their receipt of quality awards, outperformed companies in the same industries and of similar size in key financial areas, including stock performance. The study suggests that using quality awards to determine management quality is a reasonably reliable way to test managerial competence.

General Securities expanded the measure of management quality to cover recognition for the various elements that make up a management system. Its early results with the Q-100 suggest that such an approach is reasonably reliable: The stock of the companies Mark and Craig have identified as having quality management systems is returning more to investors than the stock of all companies in the S&P pool. Or put another way, their screen for managerial competence results in a group of companies that outperforms the S&P 500 primarily because of the quality of their management.

The Correlation between Quality Management and Financial Performance

A third way to determine whether a quality test of managerial competence is reasonably reliable is to look within a company itself to see if improvements in the quality of its management system correlate with improvements in its financial performance. If, for example, a company increases its profits in step with improvements in the quality of its management system, then managerial competence could be considered a contributing factor to financial performance, and a quality screen would seem to be a reasonably reliable test of managerial competence.

With that correlation in mind, consider the performance of Honeywell. Until it merged with AlliedSignal in 1999, Honeywell was an $8 billion worldwide business offering control products for the home, industry, and space and aviation. Since the early 1990s its business units had been conducting annual assessments using the Baldrige model as part of their quality improvement process, which it calls Honeywell Quality Value (HQV). Like the national Baldrige process, each business unit submitted an application that responded to the Baldrige criteria. An internal team of examiners evaluated each application, verifying its contents during a visit to the unit's site. The examiner team then provided the unit with feedback that described the strengths and areas for improvement it had found. The team also scored the application.

The Baldrige criteria include a scoring element to help companies track their progress and to help judges select award finalists and winners. Each of the seven Baldrige categories is worth a certain number of points that add up to 1,000 possible points for all categories. Honeywell kept track of the average score for all business units that applied each year, starting in 1994. This average score, along with key financial results, has been available through Honeywell's annual reports.

Figures 2.4 through 2.7 show improvements in these average scores from 1994 through 1998 correlated with four key financial

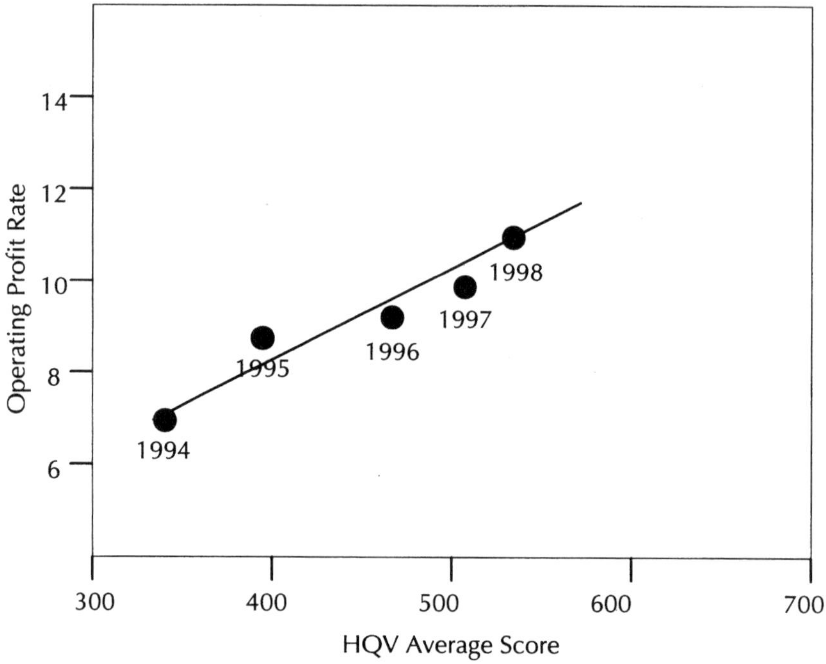

Figure 2.4 **Correlation between Average Honeywell Quality Value (HQV) Scores and Operating Profit**

measures: operating profit, earnings per share, sales per employee, and controlled working capital. Each bullet marks the point where the average HQV score intersects with performance in the financial measure for that year. In every case, as the HQV score improves, so does the financial measure.

Based on the strong correlation between its average HQV scores and its key financial measures, Honeywell concluded that HQV scores acted as a leading indicator of the changes in financial performance it could expect. Since the Honeywell Quality Value is built upon the Baldrige model, another conclusion from Honeywell's experience is that improvements in a company's quality management system, as measured by its improvement in a Baldrige-like assessment of that system, directly correlate with improvements in that

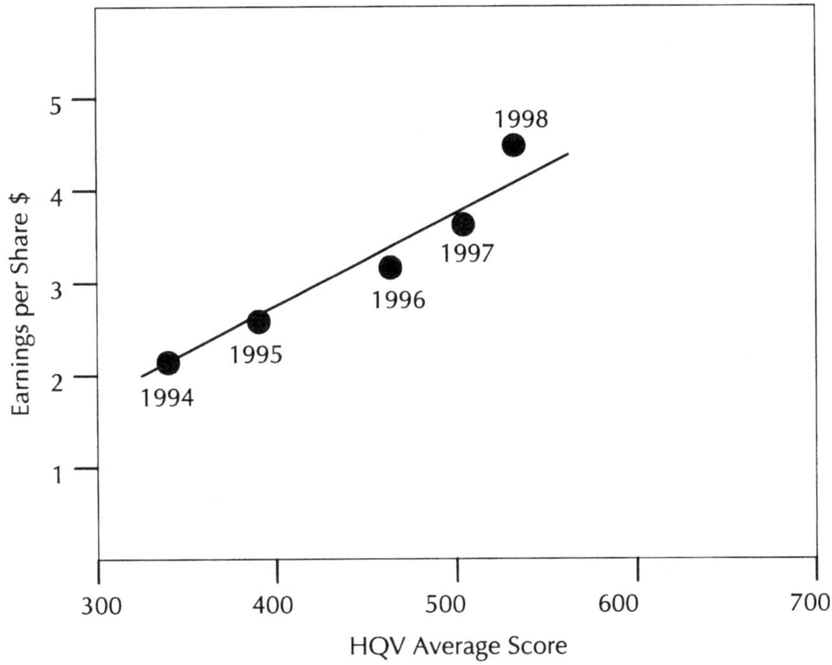

Figure 2.5 **Correlation between Average Honeywell Quality Value (HQV) Scores and Earnings per Share**

company's financial performance. Institutionalizing quality management is a reasonably reliable test of managerial competence.

Baldrige Award winners report similar parallels between improvements in the quality of their management systems and improved financial results. You will find a list of these winners, including contact information, and profiles of each at the Baldrige program's Web site at www.baldrige.org.

Why Well-Managed Companies Are Good Investments

So what do all of these charts and trends and studies mean? Basically, they mean that well-managed companies are good investments. Here's why:

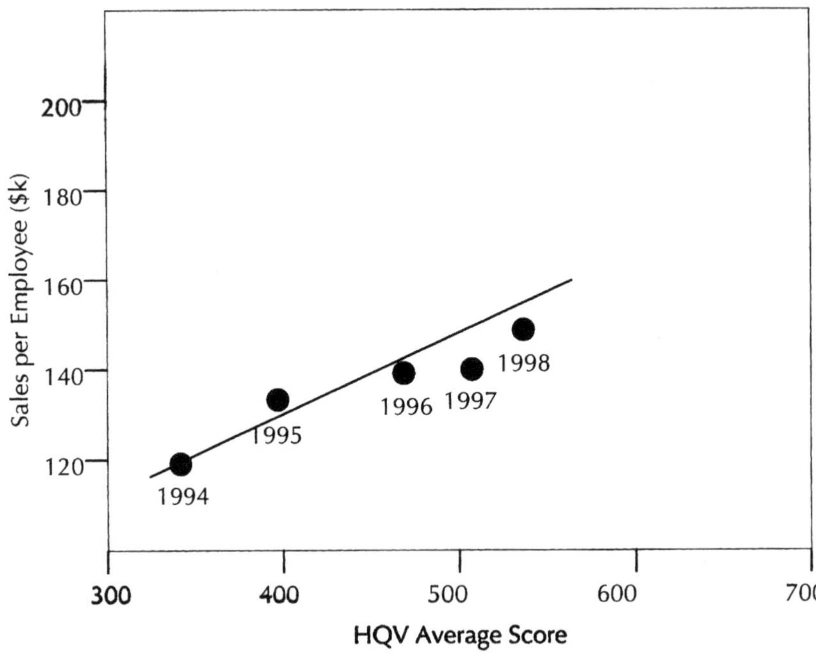

Figure 2.6 **Correlation between Average Honeywell Quality Value (HQV) Scores and Sales per Employee**

- *Managerial competence impacts a company's stock performance.* The Q-100 confirms what Benjamin Graham proposed nearly 50 years ago.
- *Companies that improve the quality of their management systems are improving their managerial competence.* The Q-100 and the study by Hendricks and Singhal provide a reliable test of managerial competence.
- *The Baldrige model and criteria provide companies with a systematic approach they can use to improve the quality of their management systems and their financial performance.* The experiences of Honeywell and other quality leaders reveal a path any company can follow to improve its managerial competence.

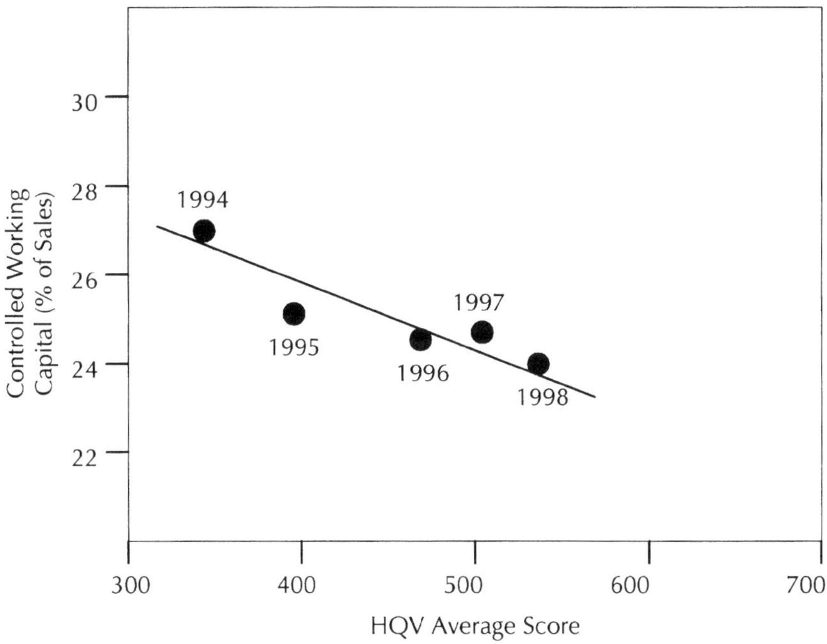

Figure 2.7 **Correlation between Average Honeywell Quality Value (HQV) Scores and Controlled Working Capital**

- *When you can assess the quality of a company's management system, you will have an objective, quantitative, and reasonably reliable test of its managerial competence.* You'll also have a tool you can use to make better investment decisions.

The next step, then, is to learn how to assess the quality of a company's management system. Before you can do that, you need to know a little about the makeup of such a system. As you will discover when you do your own research, the indicators of quality management can be easy to find, such as on the lists of certified suppliers published by a well-managed company, or they can lurk in unexpected places, like a magazine article in which an executive mentions that his company is implementing Six Sigma.

The next two chapters introduce you to the signs of quality management. Once you know what to look for, you'll find yourself reading articles about companies or watching television interviews with executives with a different purpose. You're a detective in search of clues about a company's managerial competence—only now, you know exactly what you're looking for.

Chapter 3

What Makes a Well-Managed Company: People

Most companies start with a few people and an idea—Michael Dell selling direct as a college freshman; Hewlett and Packard and their garage; Henry Ford; Amazon.com's Jeff Bezos.

When people start a company, they have no idea what it will become. They make goods or services, find customers, sell, make some more, sell some more, and soon they're adding people. Now, instead of doing everything themselves, they're delegating. They're managing. They're losing control.

A management system emerges. At first it's very informal and easy to manage: If there's a problem, you walk a few steps to the person responsible and talk about what to do next. Everybody knows everybody, decisions happen quickly, and you can see at any moment exactly how your young company is doing.

If it's doing well, the company grows. People separate into divisions and departments. Branches spring up in distant cities. Policies and procedures replace the casual culture. The entrepreneurial organization becomes a more mature company driven by a complex management system.

Complex, but rarely high quality, because for most companies the management system is an afterthought, a hodge-podge of things that worked when the company was smaller and things dictated by executives-with-a-plan and things added in desperation. A company must be focused on growth to survive, but that means it almost never takes the time to design and redesign its management system. As a result, most management systems possess a quilt-like construction made up of pieces from different eras, of different sizes and shapes, and with different intentions. It's not really a management system as much as it's a management structure, bereft of much thoughtful planning or efficient design.

That description probably fits 80% of the companies you can invest in, which is why well-managed companies have such a competitive advantage, which is why the stock of well-managed companies is such a good investment. A well-managed company achieves that lofty state by vision, design, persistence, and a lot of hard work. It's the hard work and tenacity applied to the entire organization that distinguishes a well-managed company.

Investor Beware

Now, a lot of companies and their people work hard. The fact is, a company can put up some pretty good numbers over a long period of time while enduring a mediocre management system, and that's usually due to hard work and innovation. My friend Arnie Weimerskirch calls it "unconscious competence"—you might survive for the short term but one unexpected hiccup can devastate the company.

Many factors contribute to a company's success or failure, including its management system. Despite that, as illustrated in the last two chapters, investing in a well-managed company promises a greater return than that of an average company. It's still a crapshoot, but you're stacking the odds more in your favor if you find, then invest in, quality management.

You need to be careful about a few assumptions when using management to screen your investments.

First, as I've said, management is only one factor in a company's success, although, as the evidence suggests, it's a very important factor. You may decide to invest solely in well-managed companies. Just remember that there are no guarantees attached to any strategy. Industries change. Companies merge with and acquire other companies. Leaders come and go. Unexpected setbacks occur. Well-managed companies have a better chance of anticipating and overcoming these events, but they are not immune to them.

The second caveat is that evaluating management is a fuzzy process. When it comes to a company's financial performance, you'll get widely differing opinions about what it means, but the experts tend to agree on whether a company's stock should be bought, held, or sold. When it comes to a company's management performance, almost no one agrees on the quality of that performance or what it means to investors.

Part of the problem is the absence of a universal definition of quality management. While the Baldrige model provides the closest thing, it has not yet achieved the kind of widespread acceptance that would make it the standard. *Fortune* doesn't print a quarterly list that shows American companies' management performance. The reason is not because of flaws in the model; while not everyone agrees with everything the model contains—or doesn't contain—no other management model has been so thoroughly studied and improved, so broadly dispersed, and so widely acclaimed. The reason the Baldrige model is not the universal standard for quality management systems is that not enough opinion leaders pay enough attention to the quality of management systems to endorse any model. If you ask leaders who understand management systems, the Baldrige model wins hands down.

What this means for investors is no black-and-white conclusions. Even companies that win the Baldrige Award have their problems, and they surely have the best management systems in the country. The perfect Baldrige score is 1,000 points. Baldrige Award winners receive around 700 points, meaning they still have areas to improve. In comparison, the first time most companies apply for the Baldrige Award they're lucky to score 250 points. The low score often jolts these wannabes into reconsidering just how good they are or abandoning the Baldrige process in favor of comfortable old business-as-usual.

The low score warns investors of the dangers of another

assumption, which is believing that a company actually lives up to its reputation for quality, or that a company that achieves quality in one area possesses a quality management system.

Here's an example. I've been working with a medical products company that manufactures some of the highest-quality products on the market, products preferred by doctors and patients alike. It boasts a well-deserved reputation for quality. To maintain that reputation, its production people may scrap a third of what they make because of defects. A quality management system could not tolerate that amount of waste, which indicates serious problems with supplied components, product design, or manufacturing processes. An investor who sees quality products and assumes that they prove the existence of a quality management system exposes himself or herself to added risk.

The same caveat applies to every Indicator of Quality (IQ) identified in this and the next chapter. You cannot assume, just because a company exhibits world-class performance in one area or in a few areas, that it is a well-managed company. It may be, or it may not. That's why, if you want to screen potential investments for managerial competence, you need to find out as much as you can about the quality of its management system before investing in it.

Nearly every company in the world lays claim to quality, and in many cases, rightfully so—when it comes to something like a product or service. However, when it comes to management systems, very few deserve the quality title.

Baldrige Expertise

Since management quality is such a gray area, I thought I should take a minute to list my qualifications to be your guide. I worked with my first Baldrige Award winner in 1991 and wrote my first book on the Baldrige model in 1992. Since then I've helped three other companies win the award and have written a half-dozen state award–winning applications. I've been trained as a Baldrige examiner and conducted training on the Baldrige model. I've even written a full-blown, 50-page application for a fictitious company that one of my clients used to train its internal quality award examiners.

Over the last decade I've helped companies of different sizes and types assess and improve their performance using the Baldrige criteria, including both a small market research company and a big one, a company that provides business improvement services for its clients' employees, a power supply manufacturer, a computer manufacturer, two printed circuitboard manufacturers, a dental products manufacturer, a division of a large bank, and others. I've also written three books on the subject, allowing me access to the best practices of another 60-plus companies.

My immersion in the Baldrige model has taught me two things: (1) every company's management system is indeed a system and must be treated as such; and (2) companies that institutionalize the Baldrige model do a much better job of improving that system than those that don't.

Investors who study a company's management system through the Baldrige lens will find a clearer picture of the quality of that system.

How a Company Conducts Business

Take everything a company does, from design to production to delivery, from suppliers to customers, from senior leaders to front-line workers, and you've got the elements in a management system. Whether that system serves a hundred people or hundreds of thousands, it includes the same basic components.

The Baldrige model organizes these components into the seven categories shown in the boxes in Figure 3.1. The categories cover all of the areas that contribute to a company's performance.

For the investor, the Baldrige model offers an entry point into any company's management system. Without it, an outsider wouldn't know where to look, what to evaluate, or how the different pieces fit together. To judge the managerial competence of a

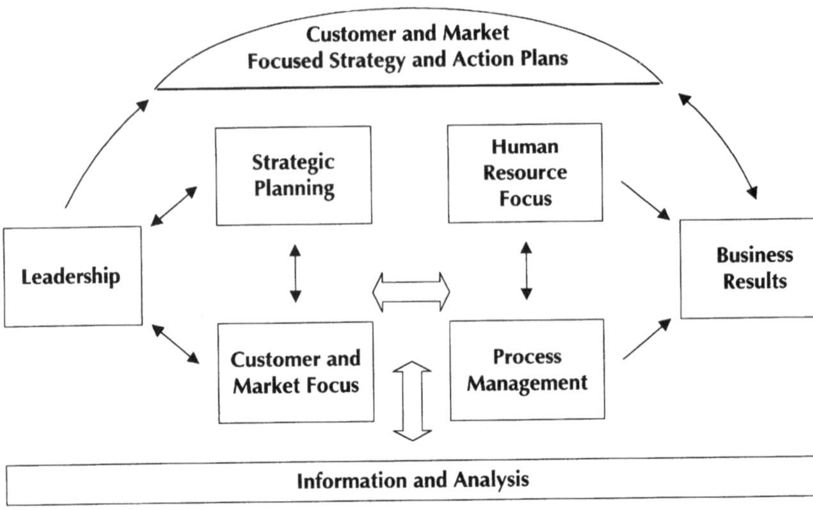

Figure 3.1 Baldrige Management Model

potential investment, you need some basic understanding of its management system and the indicators of quality for that system and its parts. In this chapter and the next, I'll introduce you to the Baldrige management system with the goal of making you fluent in the language of quality management and adept at spotting the signs of managerial competence. Once you know what you're looking for, you're already ahead of those who ignore management in their investment research and those who pay attention to management but have no clue what's important.

The first thing you need to know is that *quality management boils down to people improving processes.* I'll talk about the people side in this chapter and the process side in the next. As the key points in each category of the Baldrige system are presented, I'll explain how they define a well-managed company and where investors can look for signs that a company excels in a particular area. Each section will also include a list of Indicators of Quality (IQs), key words and phrases you can look for in your search for well-managed companies.

Leaders of Well-Managed Companies

I've yet to see a quality management system that doesn't have a quality leader at its helm. That's why leaders are important. Without a quality leader—and here I'm talking about the chief executive officer, the president or chairman or whoever is ultimately in charge—the management system will never get the attention or resources it deserves.

This isn't a natural role for most leaders. Schooled in the financial side of business and raised on meeting financial goals, they tend to lack both a systems perspective and a belief that quality, beyond product quality, is really that important to the company's success.

There are exceptions, of course. I remember a *Fortune* article a couple years ago that quoted Jack Welch as saying he thought the quality movement was a bunch of b.s. until a buddy of his, AlliedSignal's Lawrence Bossidy, told him it really worked. To his credit, Welch did some research, found value, and launched a Six Sigma initiative across General Electric (GE). He's since singing the praises of Six Sigma to the tune of $1 billion in savings for GE per year. Six Sigma is the latest-greatest thing in quality that first gained national attention when Motorola profited from it in the late 1980s. I'll explain it in the next chapter.

While these executive dabblers give quality a boost, their interest in quality management tends to fade as soon as the initial rush passes. Their short attention spans make quality a fad at their companies and the existence of a quality management system unlikely. Investors who read about a leader having a born-again quality experience may experience their own desire to buy the company's stock—just be careful to reconsider the investment when the leader's quality fervor begins to wane or when the company's leadership changes.

The leaders of well-managed companies not only recognize the value of a quality management system, they passionately and consistently promote it. They talk about it in annual reports, magazine interviews, conference speeches, internal newsletters, and any other forum they can find. When you come across comments by a company's leader, look for clues to his or her interest in the company's quality management system.

For example, in the August 31, 1998, edition of *Business Week*, an article about Cisco Systems (CSCO) pointed out that its CEO, John Chambers, "believes that the new rules of competition demand organizations built on change, not stability; organized around networks, not a rigid hierarchy; based on interdependencies of partners, not self-sufficiency; and constructed on technological advantage, not old-fashioned bricks and mortar." His beliefs reflect several of the core values upon which the Baldrige model is built, including agility, valuing partners, managing for innovation, and a systems perspective—not to mention visionary leadership. More core values can be found in the actions Chambers and his company were taking to create such an organization, including:

- Stating a strategic goal of being first or second in every market it serves
- Letting its core customers define its strategy
- Creating alliances with partners based on trust and the potential for mutual gain
- Using broad-based stock option plans to reward and retain key employees
- Involving leaders in coaching, mentoring, and communicating with employees
- Strongly emphasizing "faster, cheaper, and better"

These are not typical plans or actions most companies take, as we'll discuss in this and the next chapter. While some claim they want to be "number one," they rarely have a plan for achieving that goal. All companies would like to be "faster, cheaper, and better," but few have any systematic approach for getting there.

Yet what sets Cisco apart in this one article is the sense that it is managing the entire system. It talks about a networked organization in which leaders coach, mentor, and communicate with valued employees. This is not how most companies think.

Chambers' vision for Cisco clearly has produced results, including a phenomenal rise in its stock price throughout the 1990s. Even if you missed that early wave, if you had invested in Cisco Systems when the *Business Week* article appeared because you saw in it a confirmation of the company's managerial competence, the value of your stock would still have quadrupled over the next 16 months.

So what are we looking for when we see profiles of business leaders, interviews with them, or their speeches or writing? What are the indicators of quality leadership that can help you evaluate this critical component of an effective management system?

Indicators of Quality Leadership

The Baldrige management model considers how leaders serve their companies by:

- Defining the company's culture
- Setting priorities and expectations
- Leading performance improvement
- Encouraging learning and innovation
- Acting as role models

Defining the Company's Culture

A company reflects the personality of its leader. If all the leader can talk about is financial performance, the entire organization will be focused on short-term financial results. If, on the other hand, the leader sees financial performance as an outcome of operational performance, the organization will focus on improving the processes that produce the financial results.

There's a great story about Motorola in its hey-day. Motorola won the first Baldrige Award in 1988 with Robert Galvin as its CEO. Galvin was a quality zealot. He arranged his senior staff meetings so that quality was the first item on the agenda. After the executives finished reporting on quality issues but before they talked about financial performance, Galvin left the meeting. Since he knew exactly how Motorola was performing on its financial measures, the act of leaving was largely symbolic, but it sent a clear message about what was important to him and his company. Galvin's action helped define Motorola's culture by making quality improvement its top priority.

Leaders of well-managed companies spend a lot of time talking about all aspects of the management system that contribute to the company's growth and success. They hold out a vision for the company, preferably shared by all employees, that points everyone toward common goals. Their standard message is both broad and inclusive, extending the company's boundaries to include suppliers at one end and customers at the other. They meet with the leaders of their key suppliers. They visit their best customers. They make sure employees understand that getting and retaining customers is the company's most important work.

Within the company their message is equally broad and inclusive. They wrap everyone in the team banner, often preferring to call employees by another name, such as associates or partners. They eschew the perks that separate them and their leaders from employees. I remember hearing how Tom Malone, CEO at textile manufacturer Milliken (1989 Baldrige winner), moved his desk from a walled-in office to the middle of the floor, physically removing the barrier between himself and his people.

Leaders of well-managed companies define the culture as much by their actions as by their words. While they say training and education are important, they demonstrate the importance by continuing their education and serving as trainers. While they say teamwork is vital, they prove it by running their senior staffs as teams, recognizing team accomplishments, and listening to team reports.

The more you learn about a leader, the easier it is to figure out where he or she is coming from. Those who understand that a company is a system and that they must manage the entire system to be effective communicate their understanding through the language they use (see the Indicators of Quality [IQs]) and their active participation in the process. Those who don't understand spend their time narrowly focused on financial goals, tinkering with a system over which they have little control.

Setting Priorities and Expectations

Leaders of well-managed companies let people know what's important in clear and tangible ways. The most obvious way is through the goals set for the leaders of divisions, business units, and departments. If the primary goals are all financial, the leader is telling the organization that it must meet quarterly and annual financial targets first, and that all efforts not serving those goals are not as important. Managers and employees know that if the boss preaches quality management but only values financial performance, they'd better meet their financial goals—at any cost.

This isn't to say that the leaders of well-managed companies value financial performance any less. Rather, they have chosen to improve that performance by improving the management system that produces it. They balance their primary goals among financial, process, innovation, employees, and whatever other areas are most critical to their companies' success. Some people call this a Balanced Scorecard, which is a measurement system that helps a company carry out its strategies and improve its management system. Companies that use this approach almost always include the word "Scorecard" in their name for it, although I've also seen Scorebook, Report Card, and even Business Performance Management Matrix (3M Dental Products Division).

Leaders of well-managed companies typically set priorities and expectations through comprehensive measurement systems and through their companies' strategic planning processes. They are seeking alignment, recognizing the power generated when every work unit and employee can see how their work connects to and supports the company's mission and strategies. At Custom Research Inc., a small market research firm that won the Baldrige Award in 1996, every employee has plans and goals for the year that link directly to the company's strategic objectives. Instead of being a "blue sky" exercise that results in a book everyone ignores, strategic planning at a well-managed company is a method of cascading key messages and aligning activities.

In addition to strategic planning and measurement systems, leaders at well-managed companies establish priorities through training, rewards and recognition, and performance reviews. If you find a leader who talks about how his or her company's people are its most valuable resource, but the company provides them with ten hours of training or less per year, be suspicious of the hyperbole. Well-managed companies typically provide at least 40 hours of training per employee per year. In the year it won the Baldrige Award, Custom Research provided more than 130 hours of training per employee.

The same is true for rewards and recognition. Profit sharing, gain-sharing, and Employee Stock Ownership Plans (ESOPs) suggest that a company truly believes its employees deserve to be rewarded for the company's success.

Leading Performance Improvement

Leaders of well-managed companies tend to be personally involved in performance improvement. FedEx's Fred Smith attends his company's quarterly meetings at which employee teams share their quality success stories. He sets personal objectives with input from the board of directors. He helped develop an innovative measure of customer satisfaction called the Service Quality Index.

By these actions, Smith demonstrates to the rest of the company that teamwork and quality improvement are vital to FedEx's success, that performance improvement is a personal issue as well, and that everyone's goal is customer satisfaction and service quality.

Leaders who take performance improvement personally make it a point to share their feelings on the subject in interviews, quotes, speeches, and essays. A careful review of these and other sources will tell investors whether a company's president or CEO cares about and is involved in performance improvement.

Encouraging Learning and Innovation

When the Baldrige model was first created, it said little or nothing about learning and innovation. The term "learning organization" had not yet been coined, and the advantage to be gained through innovation was not yet fully appreciated. The Baldrige model reflected a more traditional quality approach.

The model has been refined throughout the 1990s to the point where the Baldrige core values now state that "learning needs to be embedded in the way your organization operates," and "organizations should be structured in such a way that innovation becomes part of the culture and daily work."

One of the ways the leaders of well-managed companies encourage learning is by making learning an executive responsibility. They identify the qualities or dimensions of leadership that best serve their company, then involve themselves and other key executives in acquiring the knowledge and skills they need. For example, in the early 1990s, Corning identified ten traits its leaders must have and ten more they should have. The traits included such things as being a strategic thinker and a catalyst for change, developing and communicating a rallying vision, and being financially adept. I learned about these traits in a magazine article written by Corning's CEO at that time, Jamie Houghton.

Leaders also encourage learning by participating in employee training, promoting employee development, and committing resources to comprehensive training programs. Several well-managed companies have created their own internal "universities," such as Motorola University and Solectron University, to organize and build awareness of their training activities.

Leaders encourage creativity and innovation through a similar commitment of resources. In some cases, such as 3M, the company encourages employees to spend some of their time experimenting with new ideas. 3M's leaders track the percentage of sales from products introduced in the past five years as a key measure of innovation.

Acting as Role Models

I once read a story about the leader of a Fortune 500 company who, when a member of his executive staff made a suggestion he didn't like, cried, "Air ball!" For those of you who might not be familiar with this basketball term, when a player attempts a shot that misses everything, including the rim of the basket, opposing fans like to chant "Air ball!" the next few times that player touches the ball. It's a derogatory phrase for an error that's easy to make. In my book, any leader who shows such disrespect for his executive staff is demonstrating by his behavior that people don't count for much in his company. I wouldn't invest a nickel in such a company.

Just as leaders define their companies' cultures, they also model the behavior of their people. The reason Scott Adams spends so much *Dilbert* cartoon space on the pointy-haired boss is because the boss sets the tone for the company.

The leaders of well-managed companies tend to model exemplary behavior through such activities as maintaining close contact with key customers and suppliers, pushing decisions to the people closest to an issue, treating people with dignity and respect, conducting business with integrity, and being personally involved in community service. For example, two of the traits Corning believes its leaders should have are contributing to their local communities and being active in at least one nonbusiness, nonlocal activity.

The Baldrige model expects that "an organization's leadership [will] stress its responsibilities to the public and practice good citizenship." The leaders of well-managed companies understand that their organizations operate within many communities and that it is in their best interests to support those communities.

Leadership IQs

- Shared vision
- Flat organization
- Team-based
- Industry leader
- Alignment of plans/processes/people
- Training participation
- Measurements/strategic plan cascaded
- Six Sigma
- Baldrige Award/criteria
- State quality award participation
- Shingo Prize
- *Kaizen*
- Balanced Scorecard
- Policy deployment
- Quality Steering Committee
- Benchmarking
- Best practices
- Economic value-added (EVA)
- Learning organization
- (Company) University
- 360° feedback
- Personal quality goals/measures
- Team participation
- Frequent customer visits
- Participation in customer/supplier advisory councils
- Total quality environmental management (TQEM)
- Leading corporate citizen

Employees in Well-Managed Companies

When it comes to squeezing the last ounce of profit out of a business, leaders tend to see employees as either necessary costs or profit centers, and treat them accordingly. Well-managed companies choose the latter.

As they must; business demands it. A decade of downsizing has put more responsibility on fewer shoulders. Customers expect more, whether it's better quality, quicker delivery, or lower costs—or all three. The Internet has collapsed cycle time from weeks and months to hours and days. Nobody's willing to wait anymore. If they can't get information or satisfaction from the employee they contact, they'll switch companies. If the product or service they bought doesn't meet their requirements, they'll switch companies. And if smart employees get tired of having no authority and no training and no future, they're likely to switch companies, too.

What's a company to do? Trash the hierarchy. Flatten the organization. Eliminate layers of management. Train employees, then turn them loose. Trust people to do their part in achieving the company's goals.

In her book, *World Class* (Simon & Schuster, 1995), Rosabeth Moss Kanter talks about the need for flat, fast, focused, and flexible organizations. None of this is possible without a high-performance workforce. To her list she added a fifth: fun. The days of people working primarily for a paycheck are waning as new generations seek fulfillment in their jobs. That makes fun a major factor.

Well-managed companies blur the line between work and everything else, not by expecting people to take their work home with them, but by recognizing that each employee exists outside the workplace. They have lives, and those lives affect and are affected by their work. I remember talking to an employee at Lyondell Chemical Company in Houston about her participation on a self-directed work team. At that time, her team hadn't had a manager on-site for seven years. In the book I wrote with Arnie Weimerskirch, *Total Quality Management* (Wiley, 1998), she said, "The biggest thing Lyondell has done for me has been to give me confidence and ownership. It even helps me work with my three teenagers as a single parent." This was a year after Lyondell had been recognized as one of the 100 best companies to work for in the United States.

So what are we looking for, then, when we read what employees think of their jobs and companies or when we hear friends or neighbors talk about their companies? What are the indicators of the quality employees that are essential to a quality management system?

Indicators of Quality Employees

The Baldrige management model considers how a company helps employees develop and utilize their full potential through:

- Involvement and empowerment
- Training
- Recognition and rewards
- A climate of support

Involved and Empowered Employees

While nearly every company believes it has involved and empowered employees, very few actually do. That's because the distance between an employee's traditional role (do your job and don't worry about anything else) and an employee's new role (plan your work, know your customers, measure performance, improve processes, participate on teams, etc.) is huge. Moving from traditional to new requires a deep cultural change most companies just aren't willing to make.

We all know what the traditional role looks like; most of us have worked in jobs like that. Companies that involve and empower their employees are also easy to spot. They do a lot of work through teams, including self-directed teams, cross-functional teams (people from different functions working together on a project or process), and process improvement teams (which might also be cross-functional). Their leaders stop making all the decisions, realizing that those closest to an issue are in the best position to decide a course of action. I remember talking to Larry Welliver, general manager of Honeywell Solid State Electronics Center, about the difficulty he had with this. His problem was not any reluctance to give up making the decisions, but the reluctance of those he wanted to take the responsibility to accept it. Only through his persistence did people become empowered.

Another sign of an empowered workforce is their latitude in making decisions. For example, Ritz-Carlton Hotel Company, a two-time Baldrige Award winner, empowers any employee to spend up to $2,000 to make a customer happy. No authorization required. No levels of approval. No second-guessing.

Well-managed companies also empower their employees by sharing knowledge and information. Cross-training and job rotation expose employees to different jobs and responsibilities. Open book management teaches employees how to interpret their company's financial performance, provides previously closely held financial data to all employees, and encourages them to understand how their company is doing and what they can do to improve its performance.

Companies that "open their books" to their employees signal a high level of trust in those employees, as do leaders who push decision making to all levels of the organization. Sharing information, knowledge, and decision making, along with extensive use of teams, are all signs of a well-managed company.

Knowledgeable Employees

If you studied *Fortune* magazine's 2000 list of best companies to work for, you'd find a column after each company listing training hours per employee per year. An employee at the number-one company on the list, Container Store, received 135 hours of training last year. Number-two Southwest Airlines provided 70 hours, while Cisco at number three trained each employee for 80 hours. The average for the 95 companies that reported this measure was 47 hours of training per employee per year.

Well-managed companies understand that they cannot expand the responsibilities of their employees without also expanding their knowledge. The Ritz-Carlton Hotel Company doesn't expect its front-line employees to provide world-class customer service or to make decisions about when or how to satisfy a customer's expectations without training. In their first year with the hotel chain, front-line employees receive 250 hours of training.

Training is the first step toward creating a learning organization. While there are other characteristics of a training program that can make it more effective, such as training everyone in the quality tools and problem-solving process, providing training when it is needed (called "just-in-time training" by some), and cross-training to increase employees' flexibility, most of these characteristics remain hidden to investors. Training hours is probably your most visible indicator of the degree to which a company develops knowledgeable employees.

True learning organizations exhibit more than just a penchant for training. They embrace technology because it provides real-time opportunities for learning and sharing information. Ford's plan to offer computers to all 350,000 of its employees for a few dollars a month promises to boost the company's efficiency and effectiveness by linking everyone to a worldwide network.

Learning organizations also change their physical environments to facilitate learning by removing walls and offices, reorganizing into teams, locating everyone involved in a process together, and making it easier for people to move around as new priorities emerge.

While the learning organization concept has been around for a few years, not many companies are even close to mastering it. If you hear about a company that's the benchmark for what a learning organization ought to be, you can bet it has a competitive advantage no matter what industry it is in.

Recognized and Rewarded Employees

Well-managed companies make it a point to reward their employees for their contribution to improving the bottom line through such programs as profit sharing, gain-sharing, and Employee Stock Ownership Plans (ESOPs). Hundreds of employees at growth companies such as Microsoft and Dell have become millionaires through such plans, making these attractive companies to work hard for. According to a study by Hewitt Associates and the Kellogg School of Management, the total shareholder return for companies without ESOPs was 19.2% compared to 26.1% for those with ESOPs. Sharing in the wealth they create turns out to be a great motivator.

Employee recognition, whether formal, informal, or day-to-day, is rarely apparent to an investor. For that reason, if you learn about a company being praised for the quality of its employee recognition, it's a signal that the company values its people, which is a characteristic of a well-managed company.

A Climate of Support

Well-managed companies are fun to work for even for consultants. At the quality companies I've worked with, I've found high levels of energy, enthusiasm, commitment, intelligence, and confidence. They know they're good. They know they need to get better. They know what must be done to improve. And they know their company, from executives to front-line employees, supports what they are doing.

You'll notice this cultural difference in the way a company and its people communicate. Executives talk about teamwork and the importance of people. Employees express extreme loyalty as they describe their challenging workplace, the camaraderie of coworkers, and the opportunities they have to learn and grow—much as the Lyondell employee quoted earlier in this section described her experiences.

The measures of employee satisfaction and loyalty are harder to find in public media. Few companies share the results of their employee satisfaction surveys. You may stumble across claims of low turnover or absenteeism, but those are about the only Indicators of Quality (IQs) for this area.

While the lack of public information makes it difficult to evaluate the quality of a company's human resource component, that quality is more visible in the way a company describes itself. Southwest Airlines made *Fortune*'s list of "best companies to work for" in part because of its profit sharing and stock option plans, but those plans merely reflect a corporate culture that values people above all else. In a book on the airline called *Nuts* (Kevin and Jackie Freiberg,

Broadway Books, 1996), the authors include a message chairman Herb Kelleher wrote to his employees a few years ago:

> When you're sitting around with your grandchildren, I want you to be able to tell them that being connected to Southwest Airlines was one of the finest things that ever happened to you in your entire life. I want you to be able to say, "Southwest Airlines ennobled and enriched my life; it made me better, and bigger, and stronger than I ever could have been alone."

Such statements capture the value a company places on its employees, which is surely a reason the value of Southwest Airlines' stock increased tenfold during the 1990s.

Southwest Airlines' symbol on the New York Stock Exchange is LUV.

Employee IQs

- High-performance work teams
- Self-directed work teams
- Cross-functional teams
- Process improvement teams
- Quality improvement teams
- Job rotation
- Job classification
- Open book management
- Employee development plans
- Career planning
- Cross-training
- Problem-solving process training
- Quality tools training
- Just-in-time training
- Profit sharing
- Gain-sharing
- Employee Stock Ownership Plan (ESOP)
- Employee satisfaction survey
- Employee Assistance Program (EAP)

Customers of Well-Managed Companies

No measure of performance moves a stock price more frequently than earnings. Analysts project quarterly earnings per share that, when compared to actual performance, often trigger swings in a stock's value. Investors consider current and projected revenues in their financial evaluation of a stock.

You would think earnings per share would be a good indicator of customer satisfaction. After all, the more customers buy, the higher a company's earnings. Unfortunately, the connection is not nearly that clean. Many factors contribute to earnings, including the state of the economy, the introduction of new products, product discounts or other sales boosters, general industry trends, and product shortages. A company can no sooner make the case that growing earnings mean happy customers than it can claim that a rising stock price reflects quality management.

Profit is the measure of a company's success, and profit equals revenues minus costs. Well-managed companies systematically improve both ends of that equation to increase their profits.

Improving the customer side involves:

- Understanding what customers require
- Internalizing those requirements
- Measuring how well the company meets the requirements
- Managing customer relationships

Understanding Customer Requirements

This sounds like a no-brainer. Every company should know what their customers require. Without customers, a company ceases to exist. If a company builds cars, it must know that customers require cup holders. If it provides banking, it must understand that customers demand drive-through service. So what does a well-managed company do that the others don't?

It *really* understands customer requirements. Most companies *assume* they know what their customers want but fail to truly test their assumptions. Well-managed companies go to extremes to nail down exactly what their customers expect.

When you hear that a company has a customer advisory council that meets regularly to talk about what customers need and where the industry is going and what the company is working on, you've found a company that's close to its customers. Well-managed companies rely on customer focus groups, market research, customer satisfaction surveys, telephone surveys, transaction surveys, independent surveys, customer roundtable meetings, visits to customers, customers visiting them, competitive analysis, and other methods of understanding what their customers require. Once they think they know what those requirements are, they run the list past key customers to verify it. They never assume.

Consider Lexus. Lexus started the Lexus Owners' Advisory Forum in 1998 as a way for the engineers who are designing new cars to talk to 15 to 20 Lexus owners. The customers look at the models being designed and explain to the engineers what they like and dislike.

One of the big differences between a well-managed company and everybody else is that a well-managed company knows exactly what its customers require and constantly revisits those requirements to make sure they're still accurate. A company may have ongoing contact with its customers, but if it doesn't have a systematic process for identifying and verifying requirements it cannot know what they really want. And if a company doesn't know exactly what its customers want, it will eventually lose them.

Some companies call their process for capturing customer requirements Voice of the Customer. You probably won't be lucky enough to find such an obvious clue to a company's customer focus, but it's not hard to find customer-focused companies. For example, the March 2000 issue of *Fast Company* quotes Elizabeth Spaulding, vice president of customer satisfaction at L.L. Bean: "Today, if a customer calls and wants to return a Maine Hunting Shoe, the first thing we do is find out what that customer's expectations were when buying the shoe. Did she expect it to last 10 years? If the answer is yes, then there's no question: We'll replace the shoe. If it turns out that she expected it to last only one year, then we'll repair the shoe. The point is that the customer determines the expectation. Not us."

Such evidence of a strong customer focus can be found in articles, interviews, and personal experience. In a recent edition of *Business Week*, an article about how General Motors has begun attracting consumers' attention hints at the reason that attention waned in the first place. To stop losing market share, it plans to build cars people want. To do that, it must translate potential car-buyers' requirements into designs that meet those requirements.

Internalizing Customer Requirements

Well-managed companies internalize customer requirements by involving customers in the design process. Lexus asks Lexus owners for input on their newest designs. Dell asks key business customers for their reaction to new technologies and upgrades.

In some cases, companies invite customers to participate in their new product or service design process. Intel pulls customers into its chip design process to find out if its engineers' concepts respond to the customers' needs. Such exchanges intentionally blur the boundaries between company and customer to create a product or service that has a substantially better chance of doing exactly what its potential buyers demand.

Some companies use an analytical tool called Quality Function Deployment (QFD) to translate customer requirements into measures a company can use to determine whether those requirements have been met. These measures are further translated into internal requirements for those functions that will be responsible for designing, producing, delivering, and supporting the product or service. For well-managed companies, QFD is a sophisticated approach to cascading customer requirements throughout an organization and generating strategies focused on the customer.

Measuring Customer Satisfaction

How often should a company measure customer satisfaction? Some would argue for daily, pointing to volume of products or services sold or numbers of complaints received, but these measures aren't precise enough to tell a company whether it's meeting specific customer requirements. Such requirements generally fall into three categories—quality, delivery, and cost—with service or support frequently cropping up as a fourth. Companies that have identified specific requirements in each of these categories generally survey their customers annually to determine levels of satisfaction.

One exception is Solectron, which has tracked customer satisfaction weekly for more than 13 years. The short weekly surveys, which are returned by 80 to 90% of Solectron's customers, give scores for quality, delivery, and service. Any score below a certain level triggers a formal process for resolving the issue. In addition, managers and employees review the surveys weekly to assess how well they are doing.

Companies also determine customer satisfaction through independent research. When reputable organizations honor companies with customer satisfaction awards, it's an indicator of superior performance in this area.

Another sign of superior customer satisfaction is supplier awards and certified suppliers. Some companies, such as Boeing, Ameritech, and Xerox, publish the winners of their top supplier awards in the *Wall Street Journal*. Others will provide a list of their supplier award winners and/or certified suppliers upon request. If the list comes from a company you consider well-managed, chances are good that the companies on the list are well-managed as well.

Managing Customer Relationships

When I worked with Custom Research a few years ago I was amazed to find out that its leaders didn't pay attention to their measure of satisfied customers because the measure didn't tell them anything: They had been at or near 100 percent satisfied for so long that the measure was meaningless. Instead, they focused on the percent of *very* satisfied customers, knowing through their experience and the research of others that very satisfied customers are five to six times more loyal than satisfied customers. Companies build long-term growth by retaining loyal customers.

More than 70% of Custom Research's customers told them they were very satisfied with the company. That's a world-class benchmark to keep in mind the next time some company tries to impress you with its percentage of merely satisfied customers. And it's not limited to professional service companies. I recently worked with a building products manufacturer that could point to a similarly high level of very satisfied customers.

Well-managed companies achieve these high levels by giving their customers what they want without compromising their financial position. They manage customer relationships, from asking them what they want to involving them in product design to providing service beyond the norm. This is true of L.L. Bean and Ritz Carlton.

You know companies like this. Friends tell you about them. People refer you to them. Stories of their exceptional customer service frequent newspapers and magazines. For example, in the same issue of *Fast Company* that quoted L.L. Bean's VP of customer satisfaction, FedEx courier James Briscoe said, "You want to put yourself in their shoes, as if you were the one asking for help. Part of customer service is the great feeling that you get when you see that you've made a difference."

Well-managed companies build loyal customers—and earnings—through an intense, companywide, systematic focus on their customers.

Customer IQs

- Customer focus groups
- Customer advisory councils
- Customer roundtable meetings
- Voice of the Customer
- Quality Function Deployment
- Customers involved in product/service design
- Customer surveys
- Industry studies/comparisons
- Supplier awards
- Complaint management process
- Customer delight/loyalty/retention
- Percentage of "very satisfied" customers

Suppliers of Well-Managed Companies

As with its customers, a company's connection to its suppliers used to be at arm's length—only more adversarial. Suppliers wanted to expand their profit margins while companies, wary of being gouged, demanded cost savings. Quality and delivery became secondary concerns. A company managed the activities it could control and struggled with its links to suppliers and customers (Figure 3.2).

To be fast, flat, and flexible, companies had to change this relationship. They could no longer inspect everything they received and send back the bad stuff. They didn't have the luxury of scheduling deliveries months or weeks into the future. Quality problems with supplied parts led to quality problems with the company's products. Shipping delays and long lead-times plugged the production process, building inventory, adding cost, making it more difficult to respond to changing customer requirements.

Well-managed companies recognized the inefficiencies in doing business this way and redefined their relationships with suppliers. First, they formed partnerships with their most critical suppliers, opening up their books to clarify who was earning how much, agreeing on what each side needed for the partnership to work. They clarified expectations and requirements and established per-

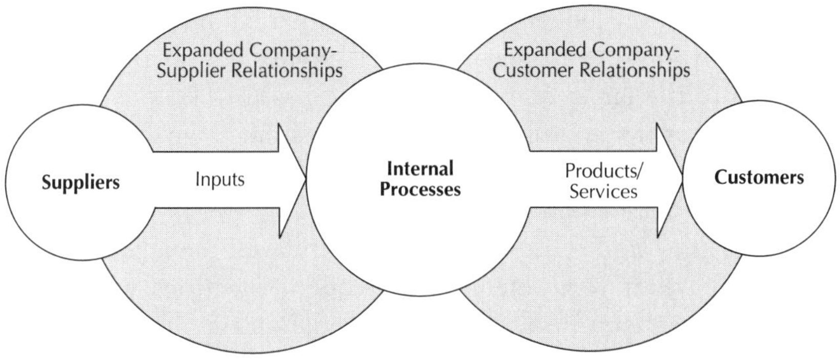

Figure 3.2 **Blurring a Company's Boundaries**

formance measures. Companies started giving their suppliers more responsibility for quality and delivery, to the point where components were being delivered for immediate use in production without ever being inspected by the company.

They didn't stop there. Well-managed companies soon realized that suppliers offered more value than just providing products and services. They were experts in their fields. They knew about new technologies and emerging trends. They understood the capabilities and limitations of their products and services. A company that could tap into this knowledge could improve its own products and services while reducing its costs.

So companies started involving key suppliers in the design of products and services. They began working with suppliers to find faster ways to introduce new technologies, to manufacture products or provide services more quickly, and to elevate quality to world-class levels.

To accomplish all of this, well-managed companies address supplier quality by:

- Evaluating performance
- Managing relationships

Evaluating Supplier Performance

Well-managed companies choose their suppliers carefully. Whenever possible, they look for evidence of similar cultures and commitment to quality management. They prefer a few high-quality suppliers to the larger numbers companies used to keep when they worried about material costs getting away from them. If you learn about a company that's drastically reduced its supplier base, that's a good sign it's focused on supplier quality.

Once they find their supplier partners, well-managed companies define their requirements in frequent meetings with these suppliers, then capture those requirements on supplier scorecards or report cards. The scorecards are typically broken up into four categories—quality, delivery, cost, and service—with performance measures for each. While companies share performance measurement data with their suppliers all the time, they formally report it monthly or, in some cases, quarterly. While not every company that uses supplier scorecards succeeds at improving supplier quality, they are an indicator that a company has a formal process for evaluating supplier performance.

Another indicator is frequent interaction between a company and its suppliers. For example, at the Dell Computer facility I assisted, key component suppliers came to the facility weekly to analyze failed components and work with Dell to ensure improvements. At that time, Dell was changing the process to return a failed component to a supplier on the same day the failure occurs to speed up analysis and correction.

Managing Supplier Relationships

Frequent interaction describes the relationship between a well-managed company and its key suppliers. Companies involve suppliers in the early stages of product and service design, tapping into their knowledge of technologies and the industry to improve their designs. They link electronically to their suppliers to speed up order entry and fulfillment, product modifications, and billing. They bring suppliers to their production floor to show how components are used and explore ways to improve the process. They meet with suppliers regularly to review performance and plans. Some even involve key suppliers in their strategic planning process. Companies that talk about their key suppliers as partners suggest the deeper relationship common to well-managed companies.

At the same time that interaction such as this has grown, the interaction around product quality has declined. Well-managed companies don't want to waste time inspecting incoming parts or scrapping materials because of defective components. They want to feel confident enough in a supplier's quality to receive material and move it directly into production without inspection. Companies express this confidence through supplier certification programs.

Goods and services from certified suppliers don't require inspection. To achieve this ideal state, well-managed companies tend to treat their key suppliers like their own employees or business units. They offer them training, include them on teams, and recognize them for outstanding performance. Some companies even have supplier representatives working full-time at the companies' facilities ordering materials with the companies' purchase orders. The concept, pioneered by Bose Corporation, is called JIT II.

As companies struggle to compete, it's no surprise that supply chain management has become a popular strategy. Well-managed companies hold key suppliers in the same regard as their own employees, finding in their suppliers the unique knowledge and skills they need to improve performance.

Supplier IQs

- Supply chain management
- Logistics management
- Supplier quality management (SQM)
- Enterprise resource planning (ERP)
- Commodity teams
- JIT/JIT II
- Supplier partnerships
- Supplier Scorecard
- Supplier report cards
- Supplier certification
- Preferred suppliers

Chapter 4

What Makes a Well-Managed Company: Processes

Say you've got a great idea for a service, a Web site maybe, and the capital to fund it. You hire designers to create the site. You work with freelancers to develop content. You contact potential advertisers to hustle banners. You buy e-mail lists and target potential eyeballs. You figure out the milestones that will tell you if the "hits" are coming fast enough, if the funding will last, if that IPO you dream about may be more than a dream.

Like it or not, your e-commerce baby is already behaving like a grown-up blue-chip. The people you and the blue-chip must have are in place: leaders (well, you), employees, customers, and suppliers. You've conducted strategic planning beginning with your business plan, then seriously revised those plans when reality set in. You've identified indicators of performance—number of hits on your new site, growth in revenue from advertising—that will help you measure progress.

And you've worked on your core processes: designing and redesigning a boffo site, changing its content almost continuously, figuring out who your best customers are and looking for more of them. The fact that you haven't thought of them as core processes only matters because it limits your ability to improve them.

All work is a process. As soon as any person or group of people start doing anything, processes are activated. The more people involved in a process, the more complicated it becomes. The number of steps increases. Decision points are added. Other functions get involved. One person's logical process becomes more formal, less logical, more bureaucratic. Things still get done but the process slows. Accountability is diffused. Costs mount.

Well-managed companies think of work as process and devote themselves to constantly improving their processes. One would imagine that this is a pretty obvious approach, but it's not. In fact, one of the easiest ways to distinguish a well-managed company from one that's not is to look for signs of process thinking.

A few years ago I helped a large market research company assess its management system using the Baldrige model. The company was beset by low customer satisfaction and extreme infighting—a culture of blameology, I called it.

I interviewed the company's senior leaders and others, asking them how they did their work, what their goals were, and how they measured and improved performance. Their answers were neither systematic nor process-oriented. If something went wrong, they blamed it on another department. If customers hated them, they blamed it on the customers. If improvements weren't made, they blamed it on incompetent people and unfavorable conditions. They worked hard, excelled at knowing their business, and cared deeply about their reputation, but they could not get past their conditioning.

The Baldrige assessment helped. The Baldrige model relentlessly pursues knowledge about processes, about how things get done. In the course of answering questions about their work, executives and managers started thinking less about blame and more about process. They began considering what steps were being taken, the redundancies, the waste, and the absence of information. Faced with no good answers to how they conducted strategic planning, determined customer satisfaction, measured performance, or managed processes, they broke through their narrow focus on visible pieces of processes to consider the whole.

Signs of new thinking appeared in meetings and conversations as people, faced with a problem, asked a new question: "What's the process?" The infighting lessened as people realized that the problems were problems with the system, not with people, and that people would have to work together to improve those processes.

Quality experts like to say that 80 to 90% of the problems a company encounters are problems with the system, not with people. When you don't understand the system, it's easy to blame people.

A business system, as defined by the Baldrige criteria, can be organized into the seven categories shown in Figure 3.1. I once asked the "father" of the Baldrige model and the first leader of the Baldrige program, Curt Reimann, why his model had seven categories and he said, "Eight were too many and six weren't enough." The fact that the seven categories have remained intact for 12 years despite dramatic changes in their content affirms his wisdom.

In the previous chapter we looked for signs that a company is adept at profiting from people, whether those people are leaders, employees, customers, or suppliers. In this chapter we'll consider how well-managed companies design, manage, and improve their processes.

Indicators of Quality (IQs) for these areas are harder to find, especially in the strategic planning area. While books have been written on the subject, like *Competing for the Future* (Gary Hamel and C. K. Prahalad, Harvard Business School Press, 1994) and *The Art of the Long View* (Peter Schwartz, Currency Doubleday, 1991), very few companies talk about what they're doing in this area.

IQs for process management and information and analysis are a little easier to find, in part because many of the TQM initiatives in the past decade have focused on this area. I'll introduce these indicators later in the chapter.

The seventh Baldrige category is totally different from the rest. While the first six ask about processes, the last category evaluates results in five areas: customer-related, financial, human resources, supplier, and operational. Investors have already been looking at financial results, although the Baldrige model is more open about which financial results are important. Results in the other areas are almost impossible to locate unless you happen to work for the company or it won a quality award and agreed to share some of them.

As I said earlier, assessing managerial competence is no slam-dunk. While that makes your job harder, it also makes the reward greater. Those investors who understand the basics of a quality management system and who keep that in mind as they read or hear about a potential investment will be better able to pass judgment on that system than the ill-informed. And that may be just the edge you need.

Planning at Well-Managed Companies

Every company plans. Even small companies think about where they're going and what they want to become. Large companies boast formal strategic planning processes that often take months to complete, making the existence of such processes almost no factor in assessing managerial competence. Whether they call it a business plan or the annual operating plan or their strategic plan, if everyone has one, it's not an advantage.

The differentiating factors appear at the front and back ends of a company's planning process.

The front end of the process is the input stage: What information feeds the plan? Well-managed companies solicit information from many sources including market conditions, changing customer expectations, new product and service opportunities, competition, risks, and human resource, operational, and supplier capabilities. Some organize these inputs into a SWOT chart (Strengths, Weaknesses, Opportunities, Threats) that highlights internal and external factors. If you happen to come across the term, it's a good sign that the company is at least considering such factors in its plan. Otherwise, you're not going to find much public evidence of quality in this area.

A few companies use scenario planning to help them shape their strategic plans. Scenario planning involves pulling together a cross-section of employees to methodically develop possible scenarios for their company's future. The goal is to imagine the different paths the future might take, identify signs that point to a particular path, then sketch in broad terms what each path means to the company and how it might plan for each one. The scenarios help shape the company's short- and long-term plans.

Some well-managed companies, like Hewlett-Packard, AT&T, Procter and Gamble, and Texas Instruments, use a process called *Hoshin planning* to identify strategies and deploy action plans. Hoshin planning originated in Japan as *Hoshin Kanri*. American companies may also call it management by policy, management by planning, or strategy deployment. Companies like the process because it promotes alignment throughout their organizations with overall goals and strategies. Actions are identified and finalized through a process called "catch-ball," which involves discussions between managers and employees, both horizontally and vertically, to agree upon how they will work together to implement the strategies.

Implementation is the back end of the strategic planning process. If a company does everything well to this stage—and there are a lot of companies that create bang-up plans—but has no proven process for implementing the plan, its strategic planning process stinks.

The problem you're going to have is finding out how well a company deploys its plan. Few clues exist. However, if you come across words like "cascading" or "alignment" in connection with strategic planning, you've probably found a company that's addressing the issue. Companies cascade their strategic plans from the top down, beginning with overall strategies that are translated into upper-level action plans that are then divvied up into plans and actions down through each business unit, division, department, function, work unit, team, and individual. Companies use processes such as Hoshin planning to align the work of every group and team with their strategic plan.

Alignment is the most desired state, and this is why: If everyone in an organization can show how the work he or she is doing directly supports the strategic plan, all energy and resources are focused on those things identified as critical to the company's success. Everyone's on the same page, to borrow a popular cliché.

One visible way companies ensure alignment is through their measurement systems. I'll talk about measurement in a minute, but the best measurement systems serve strategic plans. Each strategy includes indicators that executives can review to see how well their company is performing on that strategy. Each action includes indicators of performance on the action, indicators that align with the strategy's indicators. The most common term for these measures is key performance indicators (KPIs).

Senior leaders review performance on KPIs to see how well their company is doing on its strategic plan. Without the KPIs, leaders are guessing at performance. Without a well-deployed strategic plan, they're guessing at their company's survival.

Planning IQs

- SWOT
- Scenario planning
- *Hoshin* planning
- Strategy deployment
- Management by policy
- Management by planning
- Core competencies
- KPIs

Processes at Well-Managed Companies

While a lot of companies still believe in the value of silos, these companies are vanishing about as quickly as the family farm. In business terms, a silo is a functional group. Manufacturing could be a silo. So could Human Resources, Finance, Engineering, Purchasing, and other departments.

Silos don't work anymore. They're too slow. They're too big. They focus too much on their own success and not enough on the company's success. They don't trust each other. They lose too much in the white spaces between them.

Well-managed companies abandon their silos to focus on processes (see Figure 4.1). In most cases, they've had these processes all along. The reorganization extends throughout the company as people who used to work in functional areas switch their loyalties to process teams. Core processes are identified, such as customer service, product/service design, and supply chain management. Teams manage the processes. When no process exists or the process is too convoluted to save, a team creates a new process from scratch through an approach popularly known as reengineering, or process innovation.

As companies become more process oriented, they begin to see the weaknesses in the way they work. They involve suppliers and customers in internal processes. They eliminate layers of management and assign new roles to the remaining managers. They move quickly toward being flat, fast, flexible, and focused.

They also become agile. Agile manufacturing refers to the ability to change directions on a dime. Rather than making the same exact product for days at a time, then storing the excess as inven-

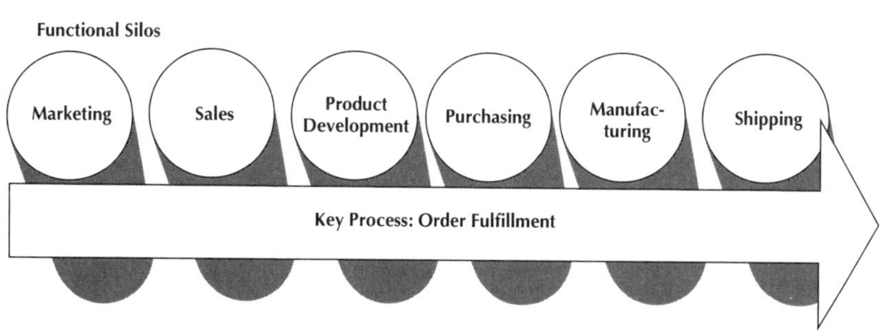

Figure 4.1 From Functional Silos to Cross-Functional Process

tory, an agile manufacturer can turn out smaller lots according to what customers have actually ordered. Agile manufacturers save the cost of large inventories. They reduce the time it takes to make products because they no longer have the luxury of long lead times. They improve quality because they can't afford to waste anything or devote time to testing it when it comes off the line. They create happier customers because customers get exactly what they want, when they want it.

Companies can do none of these things without thinking process, and that means *all* processes, not just the most obvious. If you hear about a company that's a leader in the quality of its financial processes, for example, you've probably found a rare company steeped in process thinking. Companies known for world-class human resource processes also set themselves apart from their competitors, as do companies that excel at supply chain management. More than 60% of the Fortune 1000 companies have implemented Enterprise Resource Planning (ERP) systems to their support processes.

The first stage of process thinking tends to focus on a company's most important processes: product design, manufacturing, service delivery, and so on. The second stage targets supporting processes such as finance, human resources, and sales. The final stage often leads to reorganization as support people become part of core process teams and the company directs all activities toward serving customer needs.

The ongoing effort to improve processes can take several forms ranging from *Kaizen* to Six Sigma to ISO to Baldrige, or a combination of these.

Kaizen started as a Japanese approach to continuous improvement before gaining popularity in the United States in the mid-1980s. It built on the quality circle concept, also imported from Japan, by broadening involvement to everyone in a company. While *Kaizen* continues to be taught and applied, often with significant results, it rarely attracts media attention.

The man who wrote the book on *Kaizen*, Masaki Imati, also heads the Shingo Prize for Excellence in Manufacturing. Established in 1988, the Shingo Prize recognizes world-class manufacturing practices and techniques. Past winners include such notable names as Ford, Timkin, and Lucent. Seven divisions of Johnson Controls have been awarded the Shingo Prize (NYSE: JCI).

Six Sigma

Once a company has identified its key processes, it must manage and improve them. Most of the public signs of process management relate to improving processes, including the current hot topic, Six Sigma.

The word "sigma" is a statistical measure of variation, which is the degree to which any process varies from its goal. Variation is a natural part of every process; management's inability to understand variation prevents significant and long-term improvements from occurring. Most companies operate at three to four sigma levels, enduring a cost of poor quality that eats up 15 to 30% of their sales.

In contrast, the cost of quality at Six Sigma companies is less than 10% of sales. Defect rates at these companies are around three defects per million parts compared to 6,200 for a four sigma operation and 66,800 for a three sigma company.

The Six Sigma movement started at Motorola in the 1980s, but it wasn't until the early 1990s that other companies recognized its benefits. When General Electric's Jack Welch, a long-time quality program detractor, proclaimed Six Sigma as "the most important initiative GE has ever undertaken," heads turned. When his company spent $450 million on Six Sigma projects and training in 1998, heads shook—until the savings from Six Sigma increased earnings per share by 25 cents.

Jack Welch is a bottom-line kind of guy, and Six Sigma is a bottom-line approach. The methodology can be applied to any process, as Welch proved by mandating it for all GE operations including credit card services and a television network. It directly attacks one half of the profit equation (profit = revenue – costs), and indirectly boosts the revenue side by producing more satisfied customers. AlliedSignal (now Honeywell), Texas Instruments, Crane Company, and Lockheed Martin are a few of the companies pursuing Six Sigma savings.

The heart of a Six Sigma approach is teams of highly trained employees, called "black belts," who work full-time on special projects. It's been estimated that one black belt team can save a company $1 million a year by driving defects out of key processes.

Companies that are just beginning to implement Six Sigma can expect fairly quick cost savings and profit increases. Companies with mature Six Sigma programs and black belt teams will continue to improve their bottom lines. However, it's important to keep in mind that Six Sigma, while broad in its applicability to all processes, is not a company's entire quality management system. It may cut across several of the Baldrige categories but it remains one indicator of quality.

ISO and QS

Another indicator of process management and improvement that's even more widespread than Six Sigma but narrower in its focus is ISO 9000. The ISO 9000 series is an international standard defining the elements in a quality assurance system. It can serve as a proxy for the process piece of the Baldrige model but has little relevance outside this category.

One of the benefits of ISO is that companies must register for it and be audited by an outside agency to become ISO-certified, then must pass subsequent audits to remain certified. At the very least, a company that is ISO-certified has identified, documented, and improved its key design and production processes.

In some industries, ISO certification has become a requirement to do business. American car manufacturers use a similar standard called QS to certify their suppliers. In cases where a company and all of its competitors are ISO- or QS-certified, the designation doesn't offer any advantage other than to get you into the game. However, there are some industries where ISO certification is the exception, making it a differentiating characteristic for the companies that achieve it.

Baldrige

While the Baldrige model is not a standard in the sense that a company can be certified as a Baldrige company or excluded as a supplier because it lacks Baldrige credentials, it remains the ultimate test of a management system. Companies that assess themselves using the Baldrige criteria, then act on what the assessments tell them, usually make major improvements on systemic issues that are critical to their success. Companies that internalize the model by creating their own company quality awards using the Baldrige criteria systematically improve performance, as Honeywell has demonstrated (see Chapter 2). Companies that apply for the Baldrige Award and/or state quality awards gain valuable feedback from quality experts that they use to drive further improvements.

Unfortunately, the Baldrige and state quality awards are not repeatable. Once a company has earned an award, it need not reapply the next year to retain it. For that reason, the Baldrige and state quality awards tell you at the time they are given that a company is, or is on its way to becoming, well-managed.

In many ways state, regional, and local quality awards give investors more advance notice that a company cares about managerial competence. Many states offer levels of achievement to their applicants; a bronze award winner may not have as refined a management system as a gold award winner, but its upside is probably greater. The study conducted by Kevin Hendricks and Vinod Singhal (see Chapter 1) revealed that the financial performance of companies that embrace total quality management doesn't start to perk up until a couple years after effective implementation.

Keep in mind that companies intent on institutionalizing the Baldrige model may enlist any number of the approaches described in this and the previous chapter. Motorola is a Baldrige winner and early Six Sigma advocate. Zytec won the Baldrige Award in part because of its *Hoshin* planning process. The Baldrige criteria don't prescribe how a company should operate, leaving it up to the company to determine the best course of action for its unique situation. All the criteria do are name the areas to be considered in an effective management system and provide a process for evaluating performance in those areas.

Whatever course of action a company chooses, it will need a comprehensive measurement system to review and improve performance.

Process IQs

- Reengineering
- Process innovation
- Process improvement
- Agile manufacturing
- Lean manufacturing
- Just-in-time (JIT)
- Enterprise resource planning (ERP)
- Six Sigma
- Black belts
- ISO
- QS
- Shingo Prize
- *Kaizen*

Measurement at Well-Managed Companies

How a company collects and analyzes information and data is about as hard to discover as how it plans. Yet while measurement systems used to be the least public piece of a company's management system, they've gained some notoriety lately largely due to the Balanced Scorecard.

A Balanced Scorecard translates an organization's strategies into a set of key performance measures. Executives love it because it provides them with more than just financial data to analyze. Robert Kaplan and David Norton, authors of *The Balanced Scorecard* (Harvard Business School Press, 1996), explain why financial data alone fall short. "Financial measures are inadequate for guiding and evaluating organizations' trajectories through competitive environments. They are lagging indicators that fail to capture much of the value that has been created or destroyed by managers' actions."

Kaplan and Norton identified four sets of measures or "buckets" in a Balanced Scorecard: customer, financial, internal business processes, and learning and growth. Many companies adapt the scorecard to their needs by changing the focus of these four buckets or adding new ones. As much as possible, each bucket contains a mix of leading and lagging indicators.

A leading indicator predicts performance, while a lagging indicator measures it. For example, the number of defects identified during production of a product may be a leading indicator of expected results on a customer satisfaction survey, which is a lagging indicator. The most common financial measures, as Kaplan and Norton noted, are lagging indicators.

Executives cannot effectively run a company if their only measurements are financial. It's like trying to drive while looking only at the rearview mirror, at where you've been. By the time you notice a problem, it's too late.

A Balanced Scorecard promises executives new power and insight. It addresses a major weakness in American companies, a weakness apparent to those who have evaluated scores on the first decade of Baldrige applications: U.S. companies fall short at measuring what's important to their success and are even worse at analyzing what they measure. Well-managed companies that use tools such as the Balanced Scorecard are better able to understand and improve performance, giving them a competitive advantage.

A company's goal is to identify those key performance indicators (KPIs) that tell it whether what it's doing is working or needs to be changed. The KPIs should be linked to strategies and actions identified in the strategic plan and should provide the data needed to manage and improve processes, products, and services. A company that has only financial KPIs lacks a quality measurement system.

While having a Balanced Scorecard or comprehensive set of KPIs is an indicator of quality, knowing how to analyze them is even more impressive because of the difficulty of correlating disparate measurements. The need for analysis is explained in the Baldrige criteria: "Analysis entails using data to determine trends, projections and cause and effect—that might not be evident without analysis." Rigorous analysis contributes to planning, performance reviews, process improvement, and comparisons to competitors.

The most visible signs of analysis are activity-based cost accounting (ABC) and economic value-added (EVA). Companies use these approaches to determine profit by figuring the cost of capital for their activities. Three-time Baldrige Award winner AT&T, which popularized EVA, has extended the concept to employee value-added and customer value-added.

One analytical tool well-managed companies utilize is benchmarking. "Benchmarking is the search for industry best practices that lead to superior performance," according to Robert Camp, one of this country's leading benchmarking experts. Companies that excel at benchmarking have formal processes for identifying opportunities, finding world-class performers, conducting the benchmarking, and learning from the results.

Investors can learn about well-managed companies by noticing who's doing the benchmarking and who's getting benchmarked. For example, in the September 18, 1995, issue of *Business Week*, an article entitled "Management Meccas" listed several companies that were sharing their knowledge with eager learners. Among these "corporate stars" were FedEx, GE, Microsoft, Wal-Mart, Lands' End,

Johnsonville Foods, Motorola, Springfield Remanufacturing, and USAA. Among those mentioned as benchmarking these stars were Allstate Insurance Group, Patagonia, R.R. Donnelley & Sons, Ford, and Campbell Soup.

Well-managed companies share their best practices while learning from those of others. "Almost all of these organizations have gained outside recognition, by winning plaudits from a management guru or the media, by capturing a Baldrige Quality Award, or simply by earning the admiration of competitors for solid records of profitability or revenue growth," the article states, then adds a caution. "Like any human enterprise, they can stumble, and their cult status may be fleeting." As with the other indicators of quality in this book, best practices that distinguish a well-managed company don't guarantee future success.

Business Results

The final category in the Baldrige model is business results, specifically customer, financial and market, human resource, supplier and partner, and organizational effectiveness results.

Companies that apply for the Baldrige Award must provide specific data and information showing their performance in each of these areas, and they're not going to win the award unless their results demonstrate improving trends and/or high levels of achievement. The business results category counts for nearly half of the points in the Baldrige scoring system, which means a company can seem to do everything well to this point and still not have a quality management system.

That's because the definition of a quality management system, as stated by the Baldrige criteria, is one that delivers ever-improving value to customers, resulting in marketplace success, and improves overall organizational effectiveness and capabilities. Business results are the measure of a company's ability to increase revenues while reducing costs, thus improving profitability.

Of the five areas in this section, financial results are easiest for investors to find. Market performance is harder to track down, although you might come across market share figures. The most visible customer results are awards, rating, and recognition from customers and independent rating organizations, although you may see a company tout its customer satisfaction results or customer retention rates. Human resource results are difficult to locate, with turnover or absenteeism rates the most public. Here again, awards, rating, or recognition from independent groups, such as *Fortune*'s list of best companies to work for, provide some evidence of human resource performance. Supplier performance is almost impossible for an outsider to assess unless a company publicly discusses its focus on supply chain management, supplier quality levels, or numbers of certified suppliers. The same is true for organizational effectiveness, which may be evident only when a company talks about the impact of programs such as ISO 9000 or Six Sigma, its ability to reduce the cycle time of key processes, or its industry leadership in areas such as innovation, delivery, product/service customization, and environmental quality.

When a Baldrige examiner evaluates business results, he or she studies trends for each and compares performance to industry or world-class benchmarks. Rarely can an investor do this. For that reason, you must be careful not to assume that one measurement guarantees top performance in a particular area. For example, companies like to take out advertisements proclaiming their receipt of a number-one customer satisfaction ranking by a recognized outside group. The ranking tells you that, at that point in time, the company ranked first. It doesn't tell you what the criteria were for the ranking, how the company fared in the past, whether it was first in all the subsets that contributed to the ranking, or how its competitors fared.

If this was all a Baldrige examiner had to go on, the company would not fare well in the customer results section. However, since it's often all that an investor has to go on, it at least indicates that, for this group of customers in this period of time, the company excels.

The challenge an investor faces when trying to assess the quality of a company's management system is how much value to place on the indicators of that quality. The next chapter presents a Management Screen you can use to evaluate information about a potential investment's managerial competence.

Measurement IQs

- Balanced Scorecard
- Key performance indicators (KPIs)
- Activity-based cost accounting (ABC)
- Economic value-added (EVA)
- Benchmarking
- Best practices

Chapter 5

How to Assess Management Quality: The Management Screen

Assessing management quality is far from an exact science. Consider *Fortune* magazine's 1995 list of most admired companies, which was headed by a company that also ranked first in quality of management: Rubbermaid. The value of Rubbermaid's stock proceeded to drop from $32 at the time the list was released to around $25 over the next two years before slowly climbing back to $32 by the end of 1999. Not surprisingly, the media coverage given to the company's oft-quoted and interviewed leader and its approach to management vanished except for the occasional "what happened to Rubbermaid?" article.

Those articles fought for space with ruminations about "what happened to Motorola?" Motorola, a 1988 Baldrige Award winner, ranked fourth on *Fortune*'s 1995 list with a quality of management score nearly as high as Rubbermaid's. Like Rubbermaid, Motorola's stock price languished over the next four years until it began rising during 1999.

What happened? According to the *Fortune* article that accompanied the list, most of those who responded to its survey ranked "quality of management" as a company's most important attribute.

The respondents determined management quality not by any scientific method but by perception. Reputation, it turned out, drove the score.

Without any "objective, quantitative, and reasonably reliable tests of managerial competence," Benjamin Graham pointed out 50 years ago, management "will continue to be looked at through a fog." A company's reputation doesn't pass these tests, nor do the perceptions of outside executives.

Unfortunately, as Motorola and a few others have shown, even a superior test of managerial competence like the Baldrige Award doesn't guarantee stellar stock performance—any more than, say, the expert analysis of a company's financial performance. What an objective, quantitative, and reasonably reliable test of managerial competence does is improve the investor's odds. As the Q-100 proves, a diversified portfolio of well-managed companies outperforms the average.

The Management Screen offers such a test of managerial competence. It's based on the Baldrige management model which, as I discussed in Chapter 1, meets the criteria of being objective (created by quality experts as a nonprescriptive model any company can apply), quantitative (covering all aspects of a management system), and reasonably reliable (the Q-100 and Hendricks/Singhal study correlate management quality with financial performance).

To meet these criteria, the Management Screen includes 17 statements that, taken together, describe a well-managed company. Thirty-nine questions help you determine how a company performs on the statements.

I realize that may be a lot of questions to answer for each company you're thinking about investing in, but it's not many when you're trying to realistically assess management quality. A management system is just that, a system, and any evaluation of the quality of that system suffers if pieces of it are ignored. The Management Screen gives you a way to: (1) spot the "golden nuggets" that reveal management quality as you sift through information; and (2) identify information about managerial competence that you'd like to get.

How the Management Screen Works

The Management Screen, included in Appendix A, is organized by the seven Baldrige categories: leadership, strategic planning, customer and market focus, information and analysis, human resource focus, process management, and business results.

Each of the first six categories contains two statements that describe management quality for that category. The final category, business results, has five statements addressing results in customer satisfaction, financial and market performance, employee satisfaction, supplier quality performance, and organizational performance.

Questions following each statement help assess how a company performs. The questions focus on information that an investor can get his or her hands on through newspapers and magazines, Web sites, books, and the companies themselves. In the next chapter I'll introduce these sources and explain how you can find evidence of quality management.

To help you compare one company to another or to see whether a company's management system achieves a certain threshold of quality, the answer to each question can be scored. If the answer to a question is "no" or if you don't have information that allows you to answer the question, the score for that question is "0." If you can answer the question "yes" with no reservations, the score is the most points possible for that section (scoring guidelines are given for each category). If your answer is somewhere in between—you know they do something in that area but aren't sure how good it is—the score is at or around half the possible points.

You may decide to assign more or fewer points than these guidelines. For example, if you just read where Company A's CEO launched a new Six Sigma initiative, you would want to give the company credit under "6.1 Process Management" in response to the question, "Does the company use approaches such as Six Sigma, ISO 9000, QS, or *Kaizen* to manage and improve its process?" The CEO's announcement might warrant a score of "2" because the company hasn't really used the approach yet. You may want to split the difference and give it a "3." Or you might choose to give it full credit and a "4" for implementing Six Sigma.

The fact that the CEO made it a point to talk about Six Sigma may also deserve credit under "1.0 Leadership." One of the questions in this category asks, "Do the president or chief executive officer (CEO) and other senior leaders talk about quality improvement's critical role in the company's success?" By publicizing the launch of Six Sigma, Company A's CEO has linked quality improvement to the company's success. You may want to give the company a score of "2" for that question.

How you score the questions in the Management Screen is up to you. Whether you are strict about awarding points or liberal in giving them out doesn't matter as long as you are consistent. If you're strict, a company that gets 100 of the possible 200 points may qualify as well-managed. If you're liberal, a company may need to get 150 points before you'll consider it well-managed. Assigning points is merely a way of quantifying your judgment so that you can compare different companies' management systems or better understand how a company performs on each element.

You also need to consider the source of the information upon which you are basing your judgment. Unverified company-generated publicity may be worth something, but it's probably not much. Company presidents and CEOs quoted in magazine or newspaper articles can give you a sense of the primary message they are trying to convey, but their message may not yet reflect reality at their companies. Consider the source when assigning scores.

The Management Screen is designed to help you assess management quality in 17 areas. Companies that receive the Baldrige or state quality awards deserve points in all 17 areas, with Baldrige Award winners receiving the highest possible score. During the evaluation phase, quality experts spent hundreds of hours assessing the quality of a winning company's management system. Their recommendation that it receive the Award verifies that it is a well-managed company.

State quality award winners are more problematic. State programs are not as rigorous as the Baldrige Award process. Their commitment to honoring well-managed companies is compromised by their desire to name winners that can help model the attributes state programs want to promote. I've written and read a number of Baldrige Award and state award applications; I believe the scores of state award winners average 15 to 20% lower than the scores of Baldrige Award winners. However, if a Baldrige Award winner is given 200 points on the Management Screen and a state quality award winner only 160 points, the state winner will still score higher than any company you score category-by-category.

That will be less true the less prestigious the level of state award. As mentioned earlier, most state programs offer award levels to their applicants ranging from some type of achievement award for companies new to the process to gold or crystal awards for proven, well-managed companies. A company that earns the "newby" award should be given credit for starting the journey, if for no other reason than that it may be a good investment opportunity. Score them at 50 or less, more for intent than achievement. Companies that win intermediate awards (i.e., bronze, silver) should be give proportionally higher scores.

Supplier quality awards are even harder to figure because the criteria vary. Most suppliers earn awards from customers for their performance in quality, delivery, cost, and service, which demonstrate quality management in the customer focus, process management, and business results sections, but have little to do with the other sections. You can give a supplier award winner credit either across all categories or in those three that are most relevant.

If you learn that a state or supplier award winner excels in a particular area of its management system, you can augment the "system scores" by increasing the scores for individual questions. Let's say Company B earned the Bronze Award from its state quality council and you decided to award it two points for each question in all seven categories for a total of 78 points. You then read an article in your local newspaper about Company B's exceptional new profit sharing plan, which relates to a question in section 5.1. You boost the score for that question to "4."

Ideally, your vigilance will give you enough information about enough categories to form conclusions about the quality of a company's management system. Rarely, if ever, will you be able to evaluate its performance across all categories unless the company won a Baldrige or state quality award.

How to Use the Management Screen

The goal of the Management Screen is to assess the quality of a company's management system. You are looking for Indicators of Quality (IQs) that relate to the screen's seven sections. If you don't come across anything, the score for a particular question is "0." To help you identify and credit IQs, the Management Screen asks questions that clarify the extent to which each statement reflects the way the company operates. Appendix A provides the complete Management Screen without my comments.

1.0 Leadership

The leadership section consists of two statements:

1.1 Senior leaders make quality management a top priority.
1.2 The company and its people practice good citizenship.

The first statement is one of the easiest to find information about because of the visibility of company presidents and chief executive officers. Nearly every article about a company in the mass business media quotes the company's senior leader or, in some cases, top executives. If an article focuses on the company's recent successes or bright future, you'll inevitably see why the president or CEO thinks the company is doing well. Within those comments should be clues about the presence of absence of quality management.

Three questions support the first statement:

- *Is the company guided by a single vision, focused on its customers, and promoting a work environment of empowerment and innovation?* Senior leaders of well-managed companies—especially the president or CEO—rarely say anything without reaffirming their companies' vision, their commitment to customers, and the value of employees. If they're not "talking the talk," score them "0." If you see glimpses of their conviction, score them from "1" to "3." If they seem to talk about nothing else, give them a "4."

- *Do the president or chief executive officer (CEO) and other senior leaders talk about quality improvement's critical role in the company's success?* It's one thing to claim vision, customer focus, and employee value and another to publicly link it to your company's success. If the president or CEO fails to make this connection, score it "0." If the connection is tenuous, score it "1" to "3." If the president/CEO attributes the company's present and future success to quality improvement, it deserves a "4."
- *Are senior leaders personally involved in quality improvement through such activities as conducting and taking training, recognizing exceptional performance, and encouraging learning and innovation?* Evidence of this will be harder (but not impossible) to find, and you'll probably have to settle for a less definitive answer, such as reading that Fred Smith, head of FedEx, encourages learning by attending quarterly team success story meetings or that John Chambers, CEO at Cisco Systems, involves leaders "in coaching, mentoring, and communicating with employees." If you can't find any evidence, the score is "0." If you find a little, like the Smith and Chambers examples, give the company a "2" or "3." If you find out that a company's senior leaders are truly involved in quality improvement, as you would have if you'd read about Fred Smith or Corning's James Houghton in my book, *Total Quality Management: Strategies and Techniques Proven at Today's Most Successful Companies* (with Arnold Weimerskirch, Wiley, 1998), give that company a well-deserved "4."

The second statement in the leadership category focuses on good citizenship. The Baldrige criteria state that "an organization's leadership needs to stress its responsibilities to the public and needs to practice good citizenship." Good citizenship refers to public health and safety responsibilities, business ethics, regulatory compliance, and leadership and support of publicly important purposes. Two questions support this statement:

- *Is the company considered an ethical and responsible corporate citizen?* You're more likely to come across negative information about this question than positive, especially when it concerns companies that run afoul of regulatory agencies or achieve notoriety for unethical conduct. If the company has a reputation for ethical and responsible conduct, I'd give it a "4." If you've heard nothing good or bad about it, give it a "1" to "3." If it's behaved unethically or irresponsibly, score it "0."
- *Do the company and its employees actively support their communities?* Evidence of community support can usually be found only at the local level, although some companies build a national reputation for community service. Target Stores has long been known in its hometowns of Minneapolis and St. Paul as a community champion. Now it has another champion, golfer Tiger Woods, sharing its commitment to community involvement in national television commercials. Such commitment is evident in companies that actively support their communities. When you find it, give the company a "4." Lacking definite proof but finding hints that a company cares about its communities, score it "1" to "3." If you haven't read or heard anything about the company's community spirit, score it "0."

2.0 Strategic Planning

The strategic planning section consists of two statements:

2.1 The company has an effective strategic planning process.
2.2 The company deploys its strategic plan throughout the organization.

The first statement confirms the existence of a process while the second ensures the resulting plan is deployed. Evidence of a strategic planning process will be easier to find than evidence of deployment, but information about both is still hard to come by. Three questions drill down into the quality of the process:

- *Does the company have a strategic planning process?* If the answer is "yes," score it "4." If you learn that a company has a strategic plan, assume it has a process for creating that plan and give it "4." If the answer is "no" or you don't know, give it "0"—then assign scores of "0" to the rest of the questions in this section as well.
- *Is there evidence the process involves a cross-section of employees, as is true with* Hoshin *planning, management by policy or planning, or strategy deployment?* If you discover that a company has a strategic planning process, look for clues about the quality of the process. This question asks about who's involved in creating the plan. If you see words like *Hoshin* planning or management by policy, or if you find out that employees are involved in the process, score it "4." If it sounds like the planning process involves employees but you're not sure, put it in the "1" to "3" range. If the process belongs solely to the company's executives or, more likely, you have no idea who's involved, score it "0."
- *Does the company consider many types of information when constructing its plan, such as SWOT analysis, scenario planning, or customer and supplier input?* The questions consider what feeds the planning process. Terms like SWOT analysis and scenario planning suggest an attempt to collect a range of information, as does involving customers and/or suppliers in the planning process. Score companies where this happens with "4." If you don't know what types of information the company considers, give it "0."

Creating a world-class strategic plan matters only if that plan is deployed throughout the organization. Two questions probe deployment:

- *Is there evidence the company cascades its plan throughout the organization and aligns all activities with the plan?* Evidence can be found in words like "cascading the plan" and "aligning work with the plan." *Hoshin* planning extends beyond the planning process to include deployment. If you find these terms, give the company "4." If you discover the existence of a system of key performance indicators (KPIs) or some type of Balanced Scorecard, you can probably assume they're linked to the strategic plan and award the company a "2" or "3." If no evidence exists, give it "0."

- *Does the company have key performance indicators (KPIs) or measures for tracking progress on its plan?* The presence of a system of KPIs or a Balanced Scorecard promises deployment by measuring, at all levels of the organization, what must be done to implement the plan. Give a "4" to companies with such an approach. If no evidence of deployment exists, give it "0."

3.0 Customer and Market Focus

A well-managed company has these two customer and market focus attributes:

3.1 The company delivers products and/or services that satisfy customer requirements.
3.2 The company builds and maintains strong customer relationships.

The first statement contains several important elements. Before a company can satisfy its customers, it must understand what they want. Once it knows this, it must translate customer requirements into product and services designs. To find out whether their products and services meet customer requirements, they must measure customer satisfaction. Four questions dig into these factors affecting customer satisfaction:

- *Is there evidence of processes the company uses, such as customer advisory councils, market research, surveys, and/or Voice of the Customer, to understand what its customers require?* If you find such evidence, give the company "4." However, if the only sign of a process is market research or customer surveys, there's just as much chance that there's still no formal process of defining customer requirements as there is that a formal process exists. In these cases, a "1" to "3" should suffice. No evidence earns "0."

- *Does the company have a formal process, such as Quality Function Deployment (QFD), for translating customer requirements into product and service designs?* If you find out a company employs QFD, award "4" and move on. You're more likely to find nothing about the subject unless the company's design process happens to be spotlighted in an article or you know an engineer on its design staff. Absent any information, give it "0."
- *Does the company measure customer satisfaction on a regular basis (i.e, annually, quarterly, monthly, weekly)?* You may find out a company measures customer satisfaction when it publishes results ranking it number one. If the ad identifies the frequency of its surveys, give it "4," which a company should also receive if you discover evidence of regular customer surveys in another source. Without such evidence, it gets "0."
- *Has the company received supplier awards from one or more customers?* If, like Solectron, the company has received dozens of supplier awards, score it "4." If the company has received only a few awards, or if it's not clear who gave it the awards, give it "1" to "3." No awards is "0."

Like the first statement, the second statement covers several elements. Companies build strong customer relationships through such methods as lifetime guarantees, easy return policies, satisfactory resolution of complaints, and follow-up surveys to ensure satisfaction. Their customer-focused cultures place customer satisfaction first, as Ritz Carlton does by empowering employees to do whatever it takes to make the customer happy. They target specific market segments, then do everything possible to create the most loyal customers in those segments. One question supports this statement:

- *Is there evidence the company has significant repeat business, a high rate of customer retention, and/or a high percentage (50% or above) of "very satisfied" customers?* If you come across information about repeat business, retention rates, or percentage of "very satisfied" customers, try to find comparisons to the rest of the company's industry. If such comparisons exist (usually the company will provide them) and the company's numbers are best (which is also usually the case when a company touts the loyalty of its customers), give it "4." If a high percentage of the company's revenues came from customers that also gave the company supplier quality awards or that certified the company as a supplier, the company is very likely to retain these customers and deserves "4." If you find retention rates or "very satisfied" numbers but have no way of knowing whether they're reliable, score it "1" to "3." A lack of evidence earns "0."

4.0 Information and Analysis

To help you determine the quality of a company's measurement system, this section has two statements:

4.1 The company has a performance measurement system.
4.2 The company analyzes performance measurements to assess its overall health.

The first statement is a simple switch: The company has a performance measurement system or it doesn't. The attributes of a performance measurement system are revealed in two questions:

- *Does the company use a Balanced Scorecard or other formal measurement system that identifies and aligns key performance indicators (KPIs)?* "Yes" is "5" (this is the only section with four questions, so each has a possible value of 5). Keep in mind that not every company calls their Balanced Scorecard by that name. For example, 3M Dental Products Division calls its measurement system the Business Performance Management Matrix. I've seen it called a Scoreboard or simply a Scorecard. A company may just point to its system of KPIs or key measures. If it walks like a measurement system and quacks like a measurement system, give it "5." If you're not sure, give it less. No system, no points.

- *Does the company compare its performance to that of key benchmarks such as industry leaders and world-class companies?* You're probably going to have to be lucky to find an answer to this question, but if the answer is "yes," you've found a well-managed company. Companies that can provide proof that performance on a key indicator is best-in-class, world-class, or industry-best deserve a nod, say "2" or "3." Most companies will get "0" by default.

Having a measurement system doesn't mean it's being put to good use. The second half of this section evaluates how a company analyzes the data and information it collects and uses that analysis and its benchmarking experience to improve. Two questions support the second statement:

- *Does the company analyze different types of performance measurements through such tools as economic value-added and activity-based cost accounting?* If you come across either of these terms, score "5." I'd give a company with some type of Balanced Scorecard credit here as well because the scorecard encourages analysis. Without any clear signs—which is the most likely scenario—assign "0."
- *Does the company benchmark other companies to learn best practices and improve?* Well-managed companies have a formal process for learning the best practices of other companies. This isn't the search for a number but for how other companies do things. If you learn of the existence of a formal benchmarking program, give the company "5." If you find out about

a specific benchmarking experience, such as the company learned from another company how to improve its product design process, score it "2" or "3." If no program exists or you don't know if one exists, assign "0."

5.0 Human Resource Focus

The human resource section includes two statements that explore how a company treats its employees:

5.1 The company promotes high performance by enabling employees to contribute effectively.
5.2 The company has safe, motivated, and satisfied employees.

Well-managed companies excel in three areas that promote high performance: involving and empowering employees, training them, and recognizing and rewarding them. Three questions probe these areas:

- *Does the company promote flexibility, innovation, and knowledge sharing among employees through such means as teams and cross-training?* The most obvious strategy for involving and empowering employees is teams. If you find out a company uses teams extensively, including cross-functional teams, process improvement teams, and/or self-directed work teams, it deserves a "4." A company that gives its employees more responsibility than the norm, such as Ritz Carlton empowering its employees to satisfy customers without having to get approval, also deserves a high score, as does a company that uses cross-training or job rotation to improve workers' flexibility. Open-book management or some other form of empowering employees by "opening the books" and sharing financial information should earn a company a "4" because it suggests higher levels of trust and responsibility than the average. The average, in this case, is to tell employees what to do and discourage them from thinking outside their box. Any method a company uses to break this outdated model deserves a score. If you have no evidence or the company is still stuck in the past, the score is "0."

- *Does the company invest time and resources in the training and education of its employees?* Training hours per employee has become a fairly standard measure. It says nothing about the quality, relevance, or effectiveness of the training, but it's better than nothing. If a company provides less than 20 hours per year of training per employee, give it "0." Twenty to 40 hours deserves a "1" or "2," 40 to 60 a "3," and more than 60 a "4." Other signs of world-class training might be a JIT training program (training delivered when it's needed), online training, training organized as a college/university, and extensive training in quality tools and problem solving. If you come across any of these, give the company a "1" or "2." If you hear of more than one, a "3" or "4" is in order.
- *Does the company recognize the contributions of its employees and reward them through such plans as profit sharing, gain-sharing, and Employee Stock Ownership Plans (ESOPs)?* Profit sharing, gain-sharing, and ESOPs represent only half of the equation here. If a company has any of them, give it "2." The other half of the equation is recognition, which is also much harder to detect. If you learn about a company being praised for how well it recognizes its employees (i.e., formal award programs, frequent praise in company publications, a culture of complimentary notes, which one company calls "Atta Ways"), give it at least "2" for being praised. If neither rewards nor recognition are evident, score "0."

The second statement focuses on employee satisfaction. While answers to the first statement's questions often contribute to employee satisfaction, this statement considers all the factors that create a motivated workforce.

- *Does the company publicly declare the value it places on its employees?* A company that appreciates its employees makes its sentiments public. If leaders frequently mention how important employees are, it's a sign the company values its employees and deserves "4." If you come across mixed messages, trust the negative and give it "0." Chances are good the public position has little to do with reality.

- *Do employees express positive feelings about working for the company?* As with the previous question, be wary of employee feelings orchestrated by their company. Look for the unscripted emotions of people who truly love their company, such as the Pella engineer who praised his company's "profit-sharing and bonus plans and its concern for safety" in the article accompanying *Fortune*'s most admired companies list. Companies like this, as well as companies on *Fortune*'s list, get "4."

6.0 Process Management

One sure indicator of a well-managed company is process thinking, manifest in how a company is organized, how it improves, and how it addresses problems. Two statements describe process thinking at a well-managed company:

6.1 The company systematically manages and improves its processes.
6.2 The company systematically manages and improves its supplier interactions and processes.

The first statement pretty much covers everything a company does, from talking to customers to designing, producing, and delivering products and services. Three questions delve into the depths of a company's process thinking:

- *Does the company display process thinking, as evidenced by process improvement teams, process innovation, reengineering, or other process improvements?* You'll find evidence of process thinking in such approaches as process improvement, reengineering, and process improvement teams. If such evidence exists, or if a company talks about continuous process improvement or quality improvement as the way it does business, give it "4." If the evidence is limited to a specific process, such as the product design process or strategic planning process, "2" or "3" is fair. If a company is known for blaming employees for its problems, it gets nothing; process thinking places the blame on the process, not on employees.

- *Does the company use approaches such as Six Sigma, ISO 9000, QMS, or* Kaizen *to manage and improve its processes?* In addition to the approaches listed in the question, a company that uses the Baldrige criteria to drive continuous improvement—even if it hasn't applied for or won anything—has a bona fide improvement process. If any of these is entrenched, give the company "4." If they're just starting, "1" or "2" should do.
- *Does the company include support functions such as finance, human resources, and sales in its process improvement activities?* Signs of process improvement in support areas will tend to pop up in reference to a specific function, such as finance or human resources. While you can't assume that process improvement in one area means process improvement in all support areas, for our purposes, award the company "4." It's so rare for a company to manage processes in even one support area that it deserves extra credit. Most companies will get "0" here because so little is said or written about this area—and most companies aren't doing anything in it anyway.

The second statement targets supplier processes, most notably supplier performance and supplier relationships. Two questions address these areas:

- *Does the company formally evaluate supplier performance through such methods as supplier scorecards or report cards?* The existence of supplier scorecards or report cards is an automatic "4." Supply chain management may include formal supplier evaluation, but unless it's mentioned, award the company "2" or "3." If you learn that a company has been able to greatly limit its inspection of incoming components, allows key suppliers to move materials "dock to stock," or trusts the quality of supplied materials in other ways, give it "4." If a company hands out supplier quality awards, score "4" also.

- *Does the company develop long-term supplier relationships through such activities as supplier certification, supplier partnerships, or supplier involvement on design teams and in strategic planning?* Supplier certification earns a "4." The score for supplier partnerships depends on how many and how long; if it's in conjunction with a company shrinking its supplier base, "3" or "4" is probably appropriate. Supplier involvement on design teams and/or in strategic planning signals the broad perspective of a well-managed company and deserves "4."

7.0 Business Results

Business results is the odd section with five statements, ten questions, and a possible 80 points. The large number of points is similar to the Baldrige scoring system and reflects its emphasis on results. Well-managed companies not only have excellent, well-deployed approaches in the first six sections, they also have results that prove the effectiveness of their approaches. The Management Screen asks for business results in five areas:

7.1 The company demonstrates measurable leadership in satisfying its customers.

7.2 The company demonstrates measurable leadership in its financial performance.

7.3 The company demonstrates measurable leadership in employee satisfaction, development, and performance.

7.4 The company demonstrates measurable leadership in the performance of its suppliers.

7.5 The company demonstrates measurable leadership in organizational performance.

A customer-focused company can demonstrate its ability to satisfy customers with measurable results. Two questions help you gauge its performance:

- *Does the company have data and information such as customer satisfaction survey results, customer retention rates, or independent ratings that demonstrate its customers' satisfaction?* If the company has two or more measures of customer satisfaction and they are trending upward or high, give it "7" or "8." If it only has one measure or if the measures are flat or average, give it "4" or "5." No measures, or hordes of defecting customers, deserve "0." If the company has received more than one supplier award from a well-managed company, it earns a "6" or "7." One supplier award or awards from customers with no quality credentials deserve less.
- *Does the company demonstrate customer satisfaction leadership compared to its competitors?* If the company compares its performance to that of its competitors and does better than them—and it's an independent or unbiased survey—score "8." No comparison, no points.

Of all the statements in the Management Screen, the second business results statement will be the easiest to verify. You can find financial performance data from a number of sources, track it over time, and compare it to industry averages. Two questions ask about financial and market performance:

- *Does the company show improvement or have high performance levels in financial and market measures such as revenue, profits, cash-to-cash cycle time, earnings, market position, or market share?* The second part of this question, market position and market share, will not be as easy to find as the financial data. For our purposes, if the company's financial performance is outstanding but you have no market information, score is "7" or "8." If the financial performance is good but not great and you have no market information, or if financial performance is below average but steadily trending upward, "4" or "5" will do. Good financial performance plus leading market share or growing market share deserves "8."

- *Does the company demonstrate financial and market leadership compared to its competitors?* Here again, comparisons should be relatively easy because of the wealth of financial data at your fingertips. Online comparisons are a snap at most financial Web sites. And if you happen to come across market share information, it's usually presented relative to how others in the industry are doing. If the company is leading or gaining ground in both areas, give it "7" or "8," then work down from there.

According to the Baldrige criteria, the third statement focuses on how well a company creates and maintains "a positive, productive, learning, and caring work environment." Two questions explore human resource results:

- *Does the company have data and information such as safety, turnover, absenteeism, employee satisfaction, training hours per employee, or independent recognition that demonstrate employee satisfaction, development, and performance?* You're probably not going to find more than a couple of these indicators. If what you find shows improvement or excellence, score "7" or "8." If you find results but aren't sure whether they're any good, give it "4" or "5."
- *Does the company demonstrate human resource leadership compared to its competitors?* If you find human resource results *and* comparisons to industry leaders or averages and the company looks good by comparison, award it "8." If there are few comparisons or if the company does not lead its industry, score it "3" to "5." No comparisons means "0."

The fourth business results statement claims leadership in supplier performance. Two questions seek to verify that leadership:

- *Does the company have data and information such as supplier quality levels, number of certified suppliers, or reductions in waste, inventory, or cycle time that demonstrate supplier performance?* If a company makes this type of information public, it deserves a score. If it shows improving trends or high levels, it deserves a high score. If the company hands out supplier awards, you can infer it's on top of supplier quality and give it "4" or "5."
- *Does the company demonstrate supplier quality leadership compared to its competitors?* This will be almost impossible to answer unless a company not only publishes supplier performance data but also provides comparisons for that data—and the comparisons show leadership. If all these conditions are met, award it "8." If the comparisons show the company is gaining, give it "4" or "5." But the most likely score here will be "0."

The final statement in this section asserts leadership in internal measures of performance. Since each company decides which internal measures are most important to its business, internal performance measures are not consistent from company to company. Two questions ask about how a company is performing on its most important indicators:

- *Does the company have data and information such as cycle time reduction, quality improvement, cost savings, productivity improvement, or third-party assessments (ISO, QS) that demonstrate organizational effectiveness?* Several such measures trending upward or showing high levels earn the company "8." One or two positive measures or unimpressive results deserve "3" to "5," as does ISO certification.
- *Does the company demonstrate organizational performance leadership compared to its competitors?* If it is ISO certified and most or all of its competitors aren't, give it "4." If everybody in the business is ISO certified, no score is fair. You'll probably be hard pressed to find comparisons for internal measures, so the most likely score will be "0."

With every question in the Management Screen you're looking for hard evidence of quality management. Only objective and reliable evidence of superior performance in a particular area deserves a high score, while no evidence means no score.

You'll probably find your ability to assign scores will improve the more you do it. The first time you read about a company's claim of widespread teaming or see a performance measure that looks impressive, you won't know whether the claim deserves a high score or the measure is really that impressive. More experience will give you the context you need to more confidently evaluate information and data.

Speeding Up the Process

What if you can't wait for all this management screening to be done? You're ready to put a few more bucks into stocks, you've identified a couple of promising investments, and you're eager to light that candle. Before you do, you want to see whether those promising investments might be a little less risky than they seem. You want to find out if they display any managerial competence at all—but you're not about to run the full Management Screen.

Your best bet is an online search of sites identified in the next chapter using the company names as your key words. Any evidence of quality management—which means evidence of activities and processes included in the Management Screen questions—suggests the existence of some managerial competence. You'll have to decide how much weight to give it.

Another option is to contact a knowledgeable person at a company you're interested in (see the next chapter for possible contact points and specific questions) and ask about its quality program. If the contact person says the company has one but can't name any changes, the validity of the claim is questionable. And don't buy any cop-outs about the contact person not being involved in that quality stuff. In fact, if anyone says that, I'd think the quality of their management system is highly suspect.

If you get any affirmative answers, you'll have to decide whether it's "thumbs up" or "thumbs down" for the company's managerial competence. Just keep in mind that such management analysis is only marginally better than investing in a company because it's on *Fortune*'s most admired list. To seriously assess management quality, you'll need to stick to the discipline of the Management Screen and be alert to Indicators of Quality (IQs) in what you read, watch, and hear.

Chapter 6

How to Find Well-Managed Companies

Investment guru Peter Lynch calls it "kicking the tires." A possible investment crosses your radar screen. The company is in an industry that serves consumers, such as a banking company or retail department store company. You know the name but not the operation, so you visit one of its locations, walk around, look for signs of quality.

Here's one example. A friend mentions that you ought to put some money into the stock of Kohl's Corporation, which nearly doubled in 1998 before slowing to a 17% increase in 1999. You've been in a Kohl's department store once or twice but never looked at it through an investor's eyes. While you're familiar with the name, your family always went to J.C. Penney when you were growing up and you wonder how their stock compares.

A quick stop at BigCharts (www.BigCharts.com) gives you a snapshot of the stock performance of both companies. The value of Kohl's stock has indeed trended upward, growing nearly seven times in value since 1996. The stock of J.C. Penney has lost a third of its value over the same period. The discrepancy makes you wonder what could cause one department store chain to grow while the other declines. Since both companies have stores nearby, you decide to do a little field testing.

The visit to Kohl's confirms your assumptions about the quality of its management. Aisles seem wide and inviting. Large signs guide you to various departments, most of which feature national brand clothing. You're enthralled by the variety of name brand running shoes at what appear to be excellent prices, all neatly stacked for easy access. You leave with an appreciation of how Kohl's manages its stores—and a new pair of shoes.

Your second stop isn't nearly as pleasant. Upon entering the J.C. Penney store, you decide to see if it offers the same running shoes at a competitive price, but you can't find the shoe department. No signs point you in the right direction. Racks of merchandise blend together to create a walled fortress effect. You wander through the maze, aware that there's probably something for everyone in this store but nothing that makes you stop for a second look. When you finally stumble across the shoe department, you find the shoes you just bought at the same price—but the only way you could try them on at J.C. Penney is to get a clerk to pull your size from the back room.

Returning to your car, you mentally compare the two stores based on "kicking the tires." Kohl's appears to know what it is, who it is serving, and how it will serve them. By comparison, J.C. Penney seems less sure of itself. One reflects a quality management system; the other is questionable.

As the example shows, you can make quality of management comparisons by physically checking companies out. Hands-on experience is one of several methods available to you, an approach preferred by Peter Lynch, Warren Buffett, and other investment experts who like to know something about what they're buying beyond the financial data. The more information you can gather about a potential investment, the better your evaluation of its managerial competence will be.

However, no amount of management information, like no amount of financial information, can predict how a stock will perform. All the Management Screen or other approaches to assessing managerial competence do is improve your odds by revealing well-managed companies. Yet even well-managed companies can struggle.

Well-Managed Company, Declining Stock

In the January–February 1998 issue of *Harvard Business Review*, three executives of Sears, Roebuck and Company described their company's business model. They introduced Sears' measurement system of Total Performance Indicators (TPI) focused on customers, employees, and investors. Sears used TPI to make its employee-customer-profit model operational. The model and measures helped Sears align activities within the company and deploy its management system throughout the organization.

The article was a hotbed of IQs, beginning with alignment and deployment through a measurement system of TPI and expanding to a host of indicators of quality management including:

- Strategic planning involving 150 senior leaders
- Inputs to strategic planning through five employee task forces
- Company values based on input from 80,000 employee surveys
- Employee focus groups
- Customer surveys and focus groups
- Correlating and analyzing data through causal pathway modeling
- Learning map training for all employees
- Town hall meetings to share information
- 360-degree performance reviews
- Defined leadership skills
- Sears University
- Aligning rewards and compensation
- Improvements in employee and customer satisfaction

From this article alone, you could have completed enough of the Management Screen to indicate that Sears was a well-managed company. If you had invested in Sears based on when this article appeared, the stock you bought at $45 a share in January 1998 would have been worth $62 by June of that year.

Then the decline started. By the end of 1998, Sears' stock had dropped to $42 per share. It made a modest advance in early 1999 to

$50 before plummeting to $33 by year's end. Two management shakeups in 1999 seemed to have little effect on the stock. Analysts looked at the company's 1.1% comparable store sales growth in fiscal 1998 and 1.8% growth in 1999 and found weakness, especially in the clothing lines. Discount department stores lured customers away. Specialty apparel retailers siphoned off still more, as did big-box category killers.

While Sears would surely have scored higher on managerial competence than J.C. Penney, both companies still rode in the same big, worn-out wagon. In contrast, competitors such as Kohl's sharpened their focus and gained market share. The success of Kohl's and other specialty retailers at narrowing their scope combined with Wal-Mart's and Target's success at providing a broad range of products at discounted prices redefined the market, leaving Sears and J.C. Penney stuck in an old model.

You may not want to give up on Sears quite yet, however. As an investor, if you're looking to diversify your portfolio by adding a broadline retailer, Sears, Roebuck and Company remains a good bet because of the quality of its management system. As the Q-100 has shown (and Sears is one of the 100 because of the need to diversify the index), well-managed companies, like cream, rise to the top.

If you had been looking for well-managed companies in early 1998, the *Harvard Business Review* would have provided clues about Sears, Hewlett-Packard, and General Electric. An investor's search for managerial competence often consists of two steps: seeking a well-managed company, and then, having found one, tracking down information to determine how well-managed it is.

The Internet, trade organizations, SEC filings, business magazines and newspapers, books, and other resources serve both steps. You may want to begin completing Management Screens as you identify possibilities, checking off areas as you come across information until you feel confident about a company's managerial competence. Or at least until you have enough to make an educated guess.

Armed with the Management Screen and indicators of quality

(IQs; see Appendix B), you will know what to look for during your research.

Finding Well-Managed Companies

Let's begin with how to find possible well-managed companies. Since the Management Screen and Q-100 are based on the Baldrige management model, the best place to start is with Baldrige Award winners.

Baldrige Award Winners

If quality of management is the paramount factor in your investing decision, you can't find a more objective, quantitative, and reasonably reliable test of managerial competence than the Baldrige Award process. Companies submit 50-page applications detailing what they do in all areas of the Baldrige criteria. Teams of skilled examiners evaluate and score the applications. Those that score high enough move on to a consensus phase after which, if they still score well, the companies receive a site visit. Examiners spend up to a week verifying and clarifying the application, after which they communicate their findings to the Panel of Judges. The judges debate the merits of each site-visited company before recommending their award choices to the Secretary of Commerce, who makes the final decision.

You can find the names of all Baldrige Award winners at the Baldrige National Program Office at www.quality.nist.gov, including contact information for and profiles of each. It's not a long list. In twelve years, 39 awards have been given to 37 companies (Solectron and Ritz-Carlton Hotel Company are two-time winners). Most of the award winners are part of larger companies, including Ritz-Carlton, which has been a division of Marriott International since 1997. A few are privately held, such as BI and Wainwright Industries, leaving very few well-managed, whole companies to consider.

The star of this brilliant field has to be Solectron. Not only has it won the Baldrige Award twice, it has shown that managerial competence translates into incredible financial results. For a glimpse into this world-class management system, see Solectron's Baldrige profile in Appendix D. The prevalence of IQs, especially specific measurements and trends, is truly impressive.

If you're eyeing a business unit or division that won the award with the idea of investing in its parent organization, be careful. I know from working with 1997 winner 3M Dental Products Division that one division can be an island amid an ocean of Baldrige indifference. 3M certainly qualifies as a well-managed company, but no group other than Dental Products is currently using the Baldrige model.

You also have to be wary of the lack of repeatability in the Baldrige process. A company that wins the award cannot reapply for five years. To my knowledge, only Solectron and Ritz-Carlton have chosen to do this. The lack of repeatability leaves open the question of whether an award winner continues to pursue managerial competence with the same vigor it needed to win in the first place. My experience has been that the intensity usually drops a little after receiving the Award, but the focus on performance excellence does not. The question then becomes, when is the best time to invest in a Baldrige Award winner? The short answer is *before it wins*. The long answer can be found in the final chapter.

State Quality Award Winners

At last count, more than 40 states had quality award programs based on the Baldrige model. Many simplify the Baldrige criteria by offering levels of achievement that are progressively more demanding. For example, Quality New Jersey (QNJ) offers three recognition levels:

1. The *Interest in Performance Excellence* level involves a QNJ examiner facilitating a workshop with an organization's leadership team to introduce the criteria and develop an improvement action plan.

2. At the *Involvement in Performance Excellence* level, the organization completes a self-assessment questionnaire and improvement action plan with the help of a QNJ examiner.
3. The *Progress toward Performance Excellence* level involves the completion of an abbreviated application followed by a review and site visit by a QNJ examiner team, which provides the organization with a feedback report.

There are three award levels offered by QNJ. The *Governor's Award for Performance Excellence* requires the completion of an application, a review and site visit by examiners, and a feedback report. Companies that qualify may receive a Bronze, Silver, or Gold Award.

The state award programs are the minor leagues of quality improvement; several Baldrige Award winners worked their way through state programs before stepping up to the national plate. State award programs tend to be less demanding on their applicants because they want to keep them involved while attracting new applicants. Award levels invite newcomers into the process, introducing them to the Baldrige model as the first step toward systematic improvement. Workshops and training help participants learn the criteria and how to apply them to their companies.

State quality award programs are to investors what the minor leagues are to baseball scouts: You're looking for hot prospects. While there's no guarantee that a first-time winner at a lower level will continue to use the Baldrige model, such recognition does alert you to a budding quality management effort. It tells you that the company's leaders care about understanding how their organization works and how it can improve. Since very few companies display concern about managerial competence, state award winners at any level qualify as hot prospects.

Having said that, finding hot prospects is still no simple task. The easiest way to at least identify the players would be lists at state award Web sites, but not every state program has a site. Those that do often provide scant information about their award winners, leaving an investor to wonder about a company's size, what business it's in, and whether it is publicly traded.

In an attempt to at least ease the pain of finding the state programs, I've provided contact information and, where available, links to state quality award program Web sites at www.baldrige.com.

You will notice as you scan the various state sites that some names keep appearing in different states. Companies like Solectron promote the Baldrige management model for each of their facilities as well as their companies as a whole. Local facilities pursue continuous improvement as much as an award, taking advantage of the relatively inexpensive consulting provided by expert examiners to challenge and motivate them.

Other Quality Award Winners

In addition to the Baldrige-based awards, two awards recognize manufacturing excellence: the Shingo Prize and *Industry Week*'s Best Plants.

Shingo Prize

Established in 1988, the Shingo Prize for Excellence in Manufacturing honors companies that apply world-class practices and achieve superior customer satisfaction and business results. Applicants respond to criteria similar in scope to the Baldrige criteria, with those that qualify receiving site visits. Nearly 50 U.S. facilities have won the Shingo Prize, including Federal Mogul Lighting Products, the Wiremold Company, and Milwaukee Electric Tool Corporation.

The Web site for the Shingo Prize at www.shingoprize.com lists all winners since the inception of the Prize with profiles of each. A quick browse of the profiles uncovers enough indicators of quality to verify these organizations' managerial competence.

Best Plants in America

Industry Week magazine has been honoring the "Best Plants in America" since 1989. More than 100 plants have been recognized for world-class manufacturing, including 1999 winners Dell Computer Corporation, Eaton Corporation, and Johnson Controls. At www.industryweek.com, you can find the names of all the winners and profiles that identify best practices. If you have a company name in mind, you can search the site to see if the company has any facilities on the list.

You will also find a valuable resource that may help you with the Management Screen. An article available at the Web site called "Lessons from the Leading Edge," by David Drickhamer, lists average and median manufacturing metrics, quality indicators, and workforce performance metrics for the 1999 Best Plants finalists. (Of 64 finalists in 1999, 10 were recognized as Best Plants.) Say you're looking at a manufacturing company as a possible investment and it claims an on-time delivery rate of 96%. Sounds good—until you see on the *Industry Week* site that the median for Best Plants finalists was 98.8%. How about a company that states an in-plant defect rate of 3,000 parts per million? Remember, Six Sigma is about three parts per million, so 3,000 doesn't sound all that hot—until you check out the Best Plants, which had an average in-plant defect rate of 9,278 parts per million. You'll also learn on the site that every Best Plants finalist cross-trained its employees and involved production workers in process-development efforts. And 92% of the finalists involved plant employees in benchmarking.

Finding Best-Practice Companies

Another source of information about possible well-managed companies is quality-related organizations on the Internet.

APQC

Another excellent resource for identifying "best-practice" companies and learning about their best practices is the American Productivity and Quality Center (APQC). Its Web site at www.apqc.org includes a link to best practices in the areas of leadership, strategic planning, customer relationships, measurement, human resources, productivity and quality, and more. Click on a "best practices" area and you come to a list of papers on the subject and some best-practice organizations for that area. For example, the measurement page lists DuPont, Metropolitan Life, and Nortel among its best-practice companies. Papers on the subject included "Complaint Management and Problem Resolution," "Best Practices in New Customer Service," and "Corporate Performance Measures."

As with the *Industry Week* site, you can also search the site for a specific company to see if it appears on any best practices list.

Best Practices, LLC

Best Practices, LLC offers research studies to corporate clients on many of the Baldrige categories and indicators of quality, including customer service, human resources, and business operations. As you drill down into each of these areas at www.best-in-class.com, you find a summary of reports, each of which usually includes a list of the companies included in the study. For example, the "Developing the High Performance Team" report listed 18 companies that were part of the study, including Motorola, Hewlett-Packard, Starbucks, Eaton Corporation, and Microsoft. If you want to find out more about high-performance teams at these companies, all you have to do is fork over $1,000 for the 139-page report. Knowing the list may not get you the detail you'd like to have to distinguish between companies, but at no cost, it's a bargain.

ASQ

Best practices are a little harder to find at the Web site for the American Society for Quality (ASQ). At nearly 125,000 members, ASQ is the largest organization of quality professionals in the world. Its monthly magazine, *Quality Progress*, regularly presents best practices related to all areas of the Baldrige model. Since the articles often include the names of well-managed companies behind the best practices, membership in ASQ may be a wise investment.

ASQ's Web site (www.asq.org) includes a search function called InfoSearch. If you go to "Browsing QIC Journals" and enter "Annual Quality Congress Proceedings" in the box, you'll find a list of presentations at ASQ's Quality Congresses for the last 10 years. I clicked on the 1999 proceedings and found dozens of articles listed. While each presents a paragraph summary of the article, it often includes the company at which the study took place. For example, I learned that Oriel, Inc. improved its strategic planning process by improving daily review meetings. I also discovered that DeltaPoint Corporation and Continental DataGraphics were able to apply advanced lean manufacturing techniques to a non-manufacturing information environment. If your goal is to develop a list of likely well-managed companies to consider as possible investments, searches such as this can build your list quickly.

ASQ also co-sponsors the American Customer Satisfaction Index (ACSI). Started in 1994, the index shows customer satisfaction scores for more than 200 companies in 34 industries and seven economic sectors. The scores are based on telephone interviews of customers who recently bought or used a company's product or service. You will find the names of the companies in the index and their scores at acsi.asq.org.

EVA, IT, and ISO

Some Web sites name best-practice companies in specific areas. Stern Stewart's EVA site at www.eva.com highlights brief stories of clients who implement EVA (economic value-added; see Chapter 4) including Herman Miller, SPX Corporation, Guidant, and Manitowoc. For a broader perspective of EVA, check out the Activity-Based Costing (ABC) Economic Value Added Internet Web Site Guide at www.pitt.edu/~roztocki/abc/abc.htm. The site offers a wealth of articles on the subject with leads to companies that are using it.

One way to assess how well a company manages information is by its use of information technology. Each year, *Information Week* analyzes and ranks companies according to their technology innovation. You can find a complete list ranking 500 companies going back to 1995 at www.informationweek.com.

You can find companies that have been ISO accredited at www.qualitydigest.com. ISO is an international standard developed in Europe that focuses heavily on documenting and improving manufacturing processes. You can search *Quality Digest*'s ISO database by industry code (SIC) to see which companies have been ISO-certified, or you can enter the name of a company to see if it's on the list.

Searching for Indicators of Quality

You can also find indicators of quality through traditional and electronic media.

Online Business Media

First off, online business media sites such as www.businessweek.com and interactive.wsj.com (*Wall Street Journal*) provide the most value if you subscribe to the magazine or *WSJ*'s online site. At *Business Week*'s site, you can look for IQs or companies in articles published in the past five years and read each article you choose. WSJ Interactive lists articles from the past month or so; if you want to go back farther than that, the site switches you to the Dow Jones Publication Library. A search of either key business and general magazines or 50 national newspapers turns up the headlines of relevant articles. Reading an article will cost you $2.95. If you want to search the Library's archives, you can skip WSJ Interactive and go directly to nrstg2s.djnr.com.

You can search *Fortune* magazine's Web site at www.fortune.com and get full text articles whether you're a subscriber or not.

Having spent a lot of time searching these sites, I've been exasperated with how few articles relate to a company's management system. When you search *Fortune* by company name, for example, you end up with a list of *Fortune* 500s sliced every possible way with maybe one article related to management. *Business Week* isn't much better.

At CNNfn (cnnfn.com), you can search past postings by key words. I entered "Total Quality Management" and ended up with a bunch of articles, including one on servant leadership (putting people first) that mentioned Southwest Airlines, Synovus Financial Corporation, and TDIndustries. Any financial site that includes business articles can be searched for IQs.

The Wall Street Transcript

Another online source that may reveal potential investments is the Wall Street Transcript at www.twst.com. The site features transcripts of interviews and panel discussions with senior executives, money managers, and analysts. You can enter an IQ and the site lists all transcripts that include the word or phrase. For example, I entered "Six Sigma" and the site identified a dozen transcripts including interviews with senior leaders at five companies. I assumed that, if a company president or CEO was talking about Six Sigma in an interview, his or her company was likely to be embracing it.

I made this assumption because I didn't want to pay to actually read the interviews. In most cases, you can read an excerpt from the interview and a profile of the questions asked, but you can't read the full text of the interview unless you're a subscriber, and that means forking over $630 for one-quarter's worth of access to all interviews and analyses or $2,290 for a full year.

I'll live with the free stuff, including another nifty bonus: If you check out an excerpt from an analyst's assessment of a particular industry, you can almost always find a few stocks the analyst is recommending. Off my list of Six Sigma hits, I clicked on an analysis of diversified industrial companies and found three names: Black & Decker, General Electric, and Motorola, with Black & Decker the analyst's hot pick. This also works well if you have the name of a company and want to find out more about the industry it's in or which companies in that industry are being touted.

SEC Filings

When public companies file reports with the Securities and Exchange Commission (SEC), such as annual reports (10-K) and quarterly reports (10-Q), they often include information about how they are improving their performance. You can search the SEC database by key word to find those companies that reference Indicators of Quality (IQs).

I use two Web sites to access SEC filings: Free EDGAR (www.freeedgar.com) and 10K Wizard (www.tenkwizard.com). Both work well, although I prefer 10K Wizard because I can search for a company and key words at the same time—Motorola, Six Sigma, scorecard, supplier awards, and EVA all in one search.

You can choose one or more IQs for your search word or phrase. For example, I tried Six Sigma and got 116 names from 10K Wizard. A similar search of Free EDGAR turned up Black & Decker, Raytheon, Ceridian, and others. At both sites, you can click on a company in the list (or summary, in the case of Free EDGAR) and find out how the word or phrase was used in its filing. I checked out Crane Company's annual report, filed on March 4, 1999, and found the following explanation: "As noted in previous reports, executive compensation is geared to our Economic Value Added (EVA) program, which rewards real achievements, not just progress toward arbitrary goals. We are also making gains through our Six Sigma program, described in last year's report. Virtually all of our companies now have one or more trained "black belts," who are focusing on improving manufacturing or business processes and training their colleagues to do the same. Such efforts, coupled with volume growth at most of our businesses, increased our overall operating profit margin from 9.7% to 10.5%. . . ."

To identify well-managed companies whose stock seems to be going in the right direction, you need a longer list from which you can extract the best investment candidates. Searching SEC filings can give you that list. I recently found the phrase "total quality management" in 259 filings, "Kaizen" had 39 hits, and "supplier awards" showed up in 17 filings. You may also want to try Balanced Scorecard, ISO, process improvement, supply chain management, lean manufacturing, EVA, ABC, *Hoshin* planning, profit sharing, ESOP, and other IQs. Several companies appear more than once on a list by virtue of talking about the same thing every quarter, and a few companies make more than one list.

Searching Print Media

Investors looking for management information use print media almost solely to identify potential opportunities. The problem with business magazines and newspapers is that very little of what they print relates to management systems. They're much more likely to talk about Microsoft's legal problems or Bill Gates' personality than Microsoft's management system. As a result, even if you happen to find an article that mentions a company on your potential investment list, the article isn't likely to enlighten you about any aspect of the company's management system.

The best way to use print media is to search for articles that relate to how companies run their business, see who's mentioned in the articles, then figure out what's being discussed. For example, in the May 10, 1999 issue of *Fortune*, Thomas A. Stewart described "value-adding knowledge processes . . . that provide a way to reach and keep profitable companies." That sounds like information that could be used to evaluate how well a company listens to and learns from its customers (3.1 in the Management Screen). Stewart describes such processes at four companies: General Electric, Wal-Mart, Kaiser Permanente, and Xerox.

DuPont, Monsanto, American Express, and Black Box Corporation appear in a *Business Week* article about employee incentive plans ("Bonus Pay: Buzzword or Bonanza," Howard Gleckman, November 14, 1994). The article chronicles Monsanto's eight-year struggle to develop a bonus plan that worked, how American Express linked its bonuses to customer satisfaction, employee satisfaction, and shareholder wealth creation, and how Xel cut production times from 30 days to 3 days, in part because its bonus pay supports team performance.

You can find quality management information such as this by skimming *Business Week* and *Fortune*, but you won't find it in every issue. Of the two, *Fortune* is the better source, although neither compares to the less frequent but more managment-focused *Harvard Business Review*. The bimonthly magazine presents leading-edge approaches in every area of a management system. Better yet, it names names.

In the March–April 1996 issue, an article titled "Learning from Customer Defections" noted how MBNA "asks every executive to listen in on telephone conversations in the customer-service area or the customer-recovery units." It pointed out how Deere & Company has nearly 98% customer retention in some areas and how USAA loses only 1.5% of its target customers per year. That's three world-class performances in one article. Later in the same issue, the magazine devotes an entire article to Caterpillar's process for partnering with its dealers.

Another source of potential investments is the up-and-coming behemoth, *Fast Company*. What started as a nice little bimonthly publication has grown to become a 500-page monthly monster. Best practices leap from its pages, but identifying the companies behind them is more difficult. The magazine suffers from the same cult of personality embraced by more mainstream business publications. If you're willing to wade through the dramatic graphics and startling headlines, however, you can find a few companies worth investigating.

For example, Whirlpool puts eight young sales trainer trainees together in a house for two months to use Whirlpool products. The training program, called Real Whirled, helps these sales trainers explain to clerks at big retail chains like Home Depot and Sears why Whirlpool's products are best. The same issue (December 1999) outlines a major change initiative at CIGNA P&C that turned a net operating loss of $275 million in 1993 into a net gain of $80 million in 1998. A key element in the change was the implementation of a Balanced Scorecard.

You can also check out your local business magazine, if you have one. In Minneapolis–St. Paul we've got *Twin Cities Business Monthly*, which is so staunchly pro-business you want to take a scissors to the next tie you see, but which can surprise you with a glimpse of management excellence. For example, the February

2000 issue featured a story about "trend teams" at Target that have helped it establish its upscale discount retailer brand. Once you've read about the process behind creating the image, you have a little more information you can use to evaluate Target's managerial competence.

When it comes to newspapers, you can't do better than scanning the *Wall Street Journal.* Not much of it pertains to management quality, but you can get a good sense of the ebb and flow of companies and industries, what management issues are being discussed, and, on occasion, how a company manages its business.

The business sections of local newspapers periodically feature quality management practices at local companies. Keep an eye out for such revelations in your local paper or search the Web sites of other newspapers to see if any well-managed companies show up.

Scanning Business Books

Books expose investors to any number of well-managed companies being featured for their best practices. When I wrote *Total Quality Management* with Arnie Weimerskirch (Wiley, 1998), I tracked down 51 companies known for excellence in at least one area of their management systems. Among the high-performance companies in the book were well-known quality leaders such as Corning, FedEx, Xerox, Ritz-Carlton, Solectron, Intel, 3M, and AT&T, and lesser-known quality upstarts including Staples, Dana, Engelhard, Eastman Chemical, Sprint, and USAA.

None of the companies' management systems was discussed, and that's the biggest limitation of most books unless you happen to find a book devoted to a single company. For example, my book described Intel's process for designing computer processors, a process that heavily involved customers at many stages. It doesn't say anything about measurement systems or strategic planning or any other element in Intel's management system. But it does suggest that Intel is close to its customers, and that's a good starting point.

Some books, like Arthur Andersen's *Best Practices: Building*

Business with Customer-Focused Solutions (Simon & Schuster, 1998), seem ready-made for management screening. A quick perusal of the book turns up American Express, Apple Computers, Baxter Healthcare, L.L. Bean, Black & Decker, Bose, Campbell Soup, Continental Airlines—and I'm only at the "C's." Skimming the chapter heads, you can quickly discover who's known for what, such as how FedEx, Corning, Dickens Data Systems, and Fingerhut understand markets and customers.

Other books make quality management a little harder to find. In *From the Ground Up* (Jossey-Bass, 1996), Edward E. Lawler III mentions in passing the names of companies involved in different indicators of quality. For example, he writes, "Motorola, Dana, Monsanto, Herman Miller, and a host of other companies have gain-sharing plans in some or all of their plants." There you go—one indicator of quality for creating motivated employees.

You don't have to buy all these books to find the clues. (Well, you don't have to buy the last two anyway.) The next time you're in your local bookstore, go to the business book section and look for books in the "Management" or "Big Business" sections that include words such as quality, best practices, world-class, or other IQs. Pause at the books, like Lawler's book, that seem to focus on the big picture. Skim the index. Look for company names or IQs. If you happen across a book about a single company, check out the table of contents to see if any main topics are indicators of quality.

Keep a notepad handy to jot down the names of those possible well-managed companies—and a credit card for the books so full of leads you feel guilty sitting in the aisle to read them.

If you just can't tear yourself away from the computer, a little surfing at Amazon.com can turn up even more candidates for the well-managed mantle. At Amazon.com, a book search using IQs such as Six Sigma, total quality management, or Balanced Scorecard produces lists of books for each. By clicking on a book in the list, you can find out not only what companies might be featured in the book, but also who's buying the book. Amazon.com calls these buying groups "purchasing circles."

Here's how it works. I entered "Six Sigma" in the site's general search field and came up with 17 books, including *Implementing Six Sigma: Smarter Solutions Using Statistical Methods* (Forrest W. Breyfogle, Wiley, 1999). A list of purchasing circles revealed some likely suspects—GE, Honeywell, DuPont, and Ford—plus others I didn't remember coming across before: Seagate Technology, Johnson & Johnson, and Johnson Controls. While their presence on the list doesn't mean these companies are implementing Six Sigma, it does flag them as potential candidates.

You can also click on a company to see what else it is reading, then choose a book from the list to see what other companies are reading it. For example, I clicked on General Electric and found a list of the ten most popular books for GE's purchasing circle, one of which was *Every Business Is a Growth Business: How Your Company Can Prosper Year After Year* (Ram Charan and Noel M. Tichy, Times Books, 1998). The book is built on two quality management principles: understanding customer requirements and leading cultural change. Among the other companies buying this book were Ford, DuPont, Electronic Data Systems, BellSouth Communications, 3M, and Rohm and Haas Company.

Learning from Fund Managers

Mutual fund managers choose stocks for their funds based on rigorous financial analysis. You can take advantage of their expert analysis by getting a list of companies in their funds, which you can then evaluate using the Management Screen.

To find which companies are in a mutual fund, enter the name of the fund in one of the SEC filings search engines, then read the annual report for the company that runs the fund. For example, I saw an article in *Business Week* about promising new Internet funds that mentioned the Enterprise Internet Fund. A search of SEC filings using 10K Wizard produced Enterprise's 1999 annual report. Paging through the report I found the portfolio of investments for the Enterprise Internet Fund, which included 65 companies in 14 sectors.

If you're more of a value or growth investor, prefer large- or small-cap stocks, or are looking to build equity or generate income, you can also just search the reports of companies such as Fidelity, Vanguard, Schwab, and others for funds that match your criteria.

How Good Is the Management at *This* Company?

Once you've found a company based on your searches, the next step is to complete as much of the Management Screen as possible for that company. Using the same sources just described, here's a six-step process for tracking down management information:

1. Search the SEC filings using the company's name. Read how it describes itself. Pay particular attention to any supplier awards it has received because they are outside endorsements of its quality management efforts. Look for the names of customers to see if you recognize any as well-managed; well-managed companies tend to demand quality management from their suppliers. In most cases, unless the company is large or in the automotive or electronics industries, you won't find much in the filings.
2. Assuming we're not talking about a Baldrige Award winner here, you can check the company's home state quality award Web site to see if the company has been recognized at the state level. If it's a large company and you know in which other states it has facilities, you can search those states' sites as well, but I'll warn you: Not every state quality award has a Web site and those that do can make it hard to find the winners.
3. If the company is a manufacturer, do a quick search of *Industry Week*'s Best Plants list.
4. Search the business media sites, including the Wall Street Transcript's, to see if the company appears and what is said about it. You can also go to your local library and scan back issues of the business magazines and newspapers.

5. Stop by the Web sites of APQC, Best Practices, LLC, ASQ, Stern Stewart's EVA, *Information Week*, and *Quality Digest*'s ISO to see if your company shows up on any of them.
6. Call the company. Ask for investor relations (or the head of quality, human resources, manufacturing [if relevant], the president). But before you do, jot down a few questions that will tell you enough to make an educated guess about the company's management system. You might want to ask:
   - *Who are your company's major customers?* If you recognize any of its customers as well-managed, the company probably has to perform to equally high standards to keep the business.
   - *What percent of your revenue comes from customers that have certified you to their quality standards or given you a quality award?* The higher the number, the better managed you can assume this company to be.
   - *Who are your company's major competitors?* You can check the performance of competitors to see how your potential investment has been faring. (You can even follow the same six steps to see if maybe a competitor's stock is a better investment.)
   - *Has your company won any supplier awards or other recognition for quality? If so, from whom?* If the company's won outside recognition for its performance, you may want to call the company it received the recognition from to verify the honor.
   - *Has your company implemented business process improvement? Six Sigma? Balanced Scorecard?* Asking about specific indicators of quality may help you probe for more information about what the company is doing.
   - *Do you involve customers or suppliers in product/service design?* Involving customers or suppliers in product or service design suggests flexibility, process thinking, and a willingness to partner.

Your success will vary when you talk directly to companies. Large companies tend to hold information tightly and must often get approval before providing anything of value. New companies usually don't have much to say on the subject. In an article on CNN Interactive ("Do Analysts Have the Jump on You," November 24, 1999), Louis Thompson, president of the National Investor Relations Institute, said, "Analysts ask more penetrating questions. Most of the questions of individual investors can be answered on [a company's] Web sites." Check out the Web site first, organize your questions, and you're likely to surprise investor relations with the quality of your questions.

You should try to verify any information you are given, since companies naturally put the best spin on things. Think of it as talking to the owner of a used car, then rely on the Management Screen, much as you'd turn to a trusted mechanic, to give you an objective view of your possible purchase.

As you can see, creating a list of companies to screen for managerial competence is fairly easy. Completing the Management Screen is much tougher. Small and/or new companies may not have much, if any, management-related information published about them. Technology stocks are particularly difficult because nearly everything written by or about them focuses on growth, with very little said about management. However, as I noted earlier, any evidence of a quality management system probably sets a company apart from its competitors, especially in industries and sectors where quality management is not the norm.

Chapter 7

Using the Management Screen

Let's recap.

1. *A quality management system is better than the alternative.* Independent studies show that companies that are noted for their quality management systems outperform similar companies that are not. Based on Honeywell's experience, improvements in a company's quality management system strongly correlate with improvements in key financial measures. And the Q-100 illustrates that screening companies according to quality criteria and nothing else produces a better performing group of companies. Once we agree that quality management is good, the next step is to figure out what a quality management system is.

2. *A quality management system can be defined.* The Baldrige model identifies the elements in any company's management system and how they fit together. Thousands of companies of all sizes and types use the Baldrige criteria to better understand how they operate and to improve their performance. Once we know what a quality management system looks like, the next step is to see which companies qualify.

3. *A quality management system can be located.* Enough tools and resources now exist to screen most companies' management systems and make some determination about their quality. By using a management screen to differentiate management systems, we can profit from investing in those that qualify as well-managed companies.

At this point, it's important to remember that the Management Screen works with every investment philosophy. Whether you prefer value, growth, or another approach, evaluating the quality of a company's management system makes you a more knowledgeable investor. It's one more factor you can take into consideration as you weigh your options.

Before you can do that, you'll need to feel comfortable both with the elements in a quality management system and with how you determine whether any of those elements exist in a particular company. You'll find the elements in the Management Screen in Appendix A, along with an explanation of the model in Chapter 5. In this chapter, I'm going to demonstrate how you can use the Management Screen and the resources introduced in the last chapter to build a profile of a company's management system.

To make the management screening as realistic as possible, I started with a list of nearly 50 companies mentioned in Chapter 6. I whittled down the list by removing most of the large, well-known companies, such as Dell, Motorola, Hewlett-Packard, Southwest Airlines, Black & Decker, GE, Wal-Mart, Xerox, Microsoft, Corning, FedEx, Intel, AT&T, and Ford. It's pretty easy to find management information about these companies because they regularly appear in online business sites and in magazines and books.

I shortened the list more by eliminating Baldrige Award winners Eastman Chemical and Solectron, then arbitrarily cut a few more to get my list to 15. I then decided to add an Internet stock to see how it would fare.

Using the resources described in the previous chapter, I looked for clues about each company's management system. I spent a lot of my time online, but also skimmed a few books and magazines. I kept the Management Screen handy to assess the relevance of the information being collected and to note when evidence of excellent performance appeared.

I used the following process to screen the management of companies in this chapter:

1. Identified the stock symbol using Quicken (www.quicken.com).
2. Searched the SEC filings using 10K Wizard (www.tenkwizard.com). For each company, I entered its stock symbol and a few key words such as quality, scorecard, Six Sigma, Kaizen, EVA, ISO, and supplier awards.
3. Searched the "quality" sites by company name: ASQ (www.asq.org), APQC (www.apqc.org), Best Practices, LLH (www.best-in-class.com), and Stern Stewart's EVA (www.eva.com).
4. If it was a manufacturing company, searched the Shingo Prize site (www.shingoprize.com), ISO database at *Quality Digest* (www.qualitydigest.com), and the *Industry Week* list of Best Plants (www.industryweek.com).
5. Searched the Domini Social Index (available by searching for Domini in SEC filings) and *Information Week* 500 lists (www.informationweek.com).
6. Searched the Wall Street Transcript by company (www.twst.com).
7. Searched the business magazines (www.businessweek.com and www.fortune.com) and *Wall Street Journal* (www.interactive.wsj.com).
8. Skimmed the indexes of a few business books and past issues of *Harvard Business Review* to see if the company name appeared.
9. Got financial information about the company using Quicken.com (www.quicken.com).

I spent a half-hour to an hour researching each of the 16 companies. The following profiles, presented in alphabetical order, summarize my findings and how an investor might use them to assess each company's managerial competence.

Black Box Corporation (BBOX)

Black Box showed up in a *Business Week* article about companies sharing their profits with employees. The company provides computer communications and networking services and related products to businesses.

A search of online sites revealed only one reference to Black Box. In its 1999 annual report filed with the SEC, the company mentions being ISO certified since 1994. It also describes how "each supplier is monitored for quality, delivery performance, and cost through a well-established certification program."

Part of the networking and communications devices industry, Black Box's revenue for the past year grew 38.4% compared to the industry average of 20.8%. Its five-year return on invested capital of 18.9% also compares favorably to the industry average of 15%. However, its revenues for the past five years grew at only 19.1% annually compared to the industry average of 31.9%.

I'd give Black Box 2 points for its bonus plan, which relates to Management Screen 5.1. ISO certification demonstrates process thinking and improvement worthy of 8 points in area 6.1 and another 8 points in 7.5. Its supplier certification program earns 8 points for 6.2 and another 8 points for 7.4. The company's mixed financial results warrant 4 points (7.2).

Based on a total of 38 points, I'd question the quality of its management system until I learned more about it. However, if I was looking for a value stock, Black Box's low price-to-earnings ratio—29 compared with the industry average of 258—would inspire me to call the company and try to find out more.

Black Box Corporation Management Screen

IQ	*Area*	*Score*
Bonus plan	5.1	2
ISO certification	6.1	8
Supplier certification program	6.2	8
Financial performance	7.2	4
Supplier certification program	7.4	8
ISO certification	7.5	8
	Total:	38

Ceridian Corporation (CEN)

Ceridian is an information services company focused on handling customer data for other businesses. I noticed it during a search of SEC filings for companies involved in Six Sigma. The reference turned up in the company's 1999 annual report. In my experience, few service companies have embarked on such an ambitious process.

Weaving through the Web sites in search of Ceridian turned up only one hit. At the APQC site, the company was named as a best-practice model for advanced benchmarking. The honor suggests that Ceridian employs a systematic and widespread process for learning from other companies, which may be one reason they've adopted Six Sigma.

Ceridian is also part of the Domini Social Index portfolio.

Ceridian's financial performance is far ahead of the industry average for return on earnings, return on assets, and return on invested capital over the past five years. While its revenue growth three, five, and ten years back falls short of the industry average, it more than doubled the average for the past year.

Applying this information to the Management Screen produces a score of 34: 4 points for corporate responsibility (Domini), 6 points for its benchmarking process (4.1 and assuming it has some type of measurement system upon which it can base its benchmarking); 12 points for Six Sigma because it is so rare in a service company (6.1), and 12 points for financial performance (7.2). If I was looking to invest in this industry, I'd want to find out about Ceridian's competitors to see how the company stacked up. If Ceridian compared favorably, I'd give its management system a thumbs up. Of course, I could also trust its inclusion in the Q-100 as evidence of a quality management system.

Ceridian Corporation Management Screen

IQ	*Area*	*Score*
Corporate responsibility (Domini)	1.2	4
Benchmarking process	4.1	6
Six Sigma	6.1	12
Financial performance	7.2	12
	Total:	34

CIGNA Corporation (CI)

I read about CIGNA P&C's major turnaround from serious losses to substantial gains in *Fast Company*. One component of that turnaround was the implementation of a Balanced Scorecard.

CIGNA P&C is the property and casualty insurance arm of CIGNA Corporaton, which also provides group life and health insurance and health care and retirement products and services. Although only one part of the whole company showed up in the article, I decided to check out the parent knowing that suspected quality in a business unit's management system neither guarantees nor rules out quality in the parent's management system.

CIGNA's best practices, according to APQC, include its expertise in reengineering (which it started using in 1989) and, for CIGNA P&C, information technology and knowledge management. CIGNA made *Information Week*'s list of top technology innovators. Best Practices, LLC recognized it for its measurement system (the Balanced Scorecard again) and for employee management and development. The latter is reflected in CIGNA's tenth-place ranking as one of America's family-friendly companies (*Business Week*). CIGNA is also part of Domini's Social Index. *Fortune* ranked it third on its Most Admired list in the health care category.

Making the Most Admired list usually indicates strong financial performance, but CIGNA's results are mixed. Its return on earnings for the last five years is at the industry average, return on invested capital is slightly better than average, and return on assets is about half the average. Its one-year revenue growth was actually a loss of 5.5% compared with the industry average growth of 0.3.

Let's see how all this might add up on the Management Screen:

- Inclusion in the Domini Social Index earns 4 points in 1.2.
- The Balanced Scorecard and supporting recognition for its measurement system and IT capabilities warrant 8 points in 4.1 and another 8 in 4.2.

- Reengineering is a demanding approach to process innovation that suggests process thinking, management, and improvement. The fact that the company's been doing it for more than a decade means it's probably been extended to support functions and supplier processes. I'd score it 12 points for 6.1 and 6 points for 6.2.
- Being recognized for employee management and development deserves 8 points for 5.1, while the family-friendly honor brings another 6 for 5.2. The honor also earns 8 points in 7.3 for human resource results.
- In the area of financial performance, I gave CIGNA 6 points for 7.2 because it deserved some credit for the Most Admired list and positive financial indicators.

That comes to a total of 66 points, strong support for the presence of a quality management system.

CIGNA Corporation Management Screen

IQ	*Area*	*Score*
Corporate responsibility (Domini)	1.2	4
Balanced Scorecard—measurement system	4.1	8
Balanced Scorecard—analysis	4.2	8
Employee management and development	5.1	8
Family friendly recognition	5.2	6
Reengineering—internal processes	6.1	12
Reengineering—supplier processes	6.2	6
Financial performance/Most Admired status	7.2	6
Family friendly recognition	7.3	8
	Total:	66

Dana Corporation (DCN)

I first learned about Dana when I wrote about Dana Commercial Credit in my book, *Total Quality Management.* Dana Commercial

Credit won the Baldrige Award in 1996, but as I just noted, you can't assume a whole company believes what one division practices—especially when that division is so different from the rest of the company. Dana Commercial Credit finances leases. Dana Corporation is known for manufacturing components for cars and other industries.

From SEC filings I learned that Dana adopted EVA in 1998. One of its plants was awarded the Shingo Prize in 1991 and most of its plants have achieved ISO certification. Three Dana facilities have been honored as Best Plants by *Industry Week*. Its gain-sharing program earned praise in *From the Ground Up* (Edward E. Lawler, Jossey-Bass, 1996), while APQC recognized employee training at Dana University as a best practice. It is part of Domini's Social Index. The company also made *Fortune*'s Most Admired list in the Motor Vehicles and Parts category.

Dana's financial performance has been at or above industry standards, with revenue growth nearly double the industry average over the last three years but at the average for the past year. Return on equity over five years is at the industry average while return on invested capital trails it slightly.

Based on these inputs, the first thing I had to figure out was how to value Dana Commercial Credit's Baldrige Award. I arbitrarily assigned it 40 points—about one point per Management Screen question—since leasing isn't Dana's primary business. The implementation of EVA relates directly to 4.2 and indirectly to 4.1 (you need good measures to be able to effectively analyze them) for a combined score of 16 points. Its presence in Domini's portfolio earned 4 points. The Shingo Prize, widespread ISO certification, and Best Plants honors suggest committed leadership (1.1), employee involvement (5.1), and process management (6.1). I'd score it 8, 12, and 10 points, respectively, with the score of 5.1 also reflecting Dana University and the gain-sharing program. I also awarded it 16 points for organizational performance (7.5) based on all the honors its plants have received.

While the company's financial performance is as good as or better than the industry average, its inclusion in the Most Admired strengthens its case. I gave it 10 points for 7.2.

My total for Dana Corporation came to 116 points.

Dana Corporation Management Screen

IQ	*Area*	*Score*
Baldrige Award: Dana Commercial Credit	All	40
Committed leadership: Shingo Prize, ISO, Best Plants	1.1	8
Corporate responsibility (Domini)	1.2	4
EVA—measurement	4.1	8
EVA—analysis	4.2	8
Employee involvement: Dana U., gain-sharing, etc.	5.1	12
Process management: ISO, Shingo, Best Plants	6.1	10
Financial performance/Most Admired status	7.2	10
Organizational performance	7.5	16
	Total:	116

Eaton Corporation (ETN)

Eaton Corporation has a lot in common with Dana, including some of its markets, manufacturing a variety of products for the automotive and other industries. Suppliers to automobile manufacturers have a tradition of high-quality standards, and Eaton and Dana uphold that tradition.

I noticed Eaton while surfing the Best Practices, LLC Web site, which recognized the company for its high-performance teams. Two books also touted Eaton's team emphasis, with *From the Ground Up* describing the company's "Excellence through People" initiative in place since 1984. The Best Practices site also honored Eaton for executive communication. APQC identified Eaton as a role model for its Baldrige self-assessment process.

The company made the *Information Week* list for technology innovation. One of its facilities was honored as an *Industry Week* Best Plant. Another facility won the Silver Maryland Quality Award. And nearly 50 of its facilities are ISO certified.

Eaton's revenue growth three, five, and ten years back has fallen short of the industry average, although its past year's performance of 26.8% well outpaced the average of 5.3%. Its return on equity, return on assets, and return on invested capital for a five-year period are all around the industry average.

Let's see how these translate into Management Screen scores. Eaton's well-substantiated team culture deserves 10 points for 5.1 and another 8 for 7.3. Executive communication and the "Excellence through People" effort indicate that senior leaders are personally involved in quality improvement, earning 8 points for 1.1. Its recognition for technology innovation translates into 8 points in 4.1.

From my experience, companies that conduct internal Baldrige assessments develop a valuable systems perspective while continuously improving their processes. Honeywell's experience provides supporting data (see Chapter 2). Since the assessment process generates improvements in all areas of the management system, I awarded Eaton 50 points, slightly more than what I gave Dana because Eaton's assessment process extends throughout the organization.

Eaton's Best Plant honor, Maryland Quality Award, and ISO-certified plants earned 10 points for 6.1 and another 16 points for 7.5. I also gave it 6 points for financial performance (7.2).

With a total score of 116 points, Eaton certainly qualifies as a well-managed company.

Eaton Corporation Management Screen

IQ	*Area*	*Score*
Baldrige self-assessment process	All	50
Personal involvement of leaders	1.1	8
Measurement system (*Information Week*)	4.1	8
Team culture	5.1	10
Process management: ISO, MD Quality Award, Best Plant	6.1	10
Financial performance	7.2	6
Human resources performance: teaming	7.3	8
Organizational performance	7.5	16
	Total:	116

Guidant Corporation (GDT)

Guidant appeared in a search of Stern Stewart's EVA site as a client that implemented an economic value-added financial management system. A scan of SEC filings revealed that the company started using EVA in 1995. The scan also turned up the existence of ISO-certified facilities. A quick check of *Quality Digest*'s ISO database showed two Guidant plants had received ISO certification.

Guidant manufactures medical devices. *Fortune* magazine ranked it second in the Medical Products and Equipment category on its Most Admired Companies list. It is part of Domini's Social Index. The company also earned a spot on *Fortune*'s 1999 list as one of the Best Companies to Work For. The list indicates that Guidant provides each employee with 53 hours of training per year. In my experience, anything above 40 hours is impressive.

Guidant's financial performance outpaces the industry across the board. Return on equity, return on assets, and return on invested capital for the past five years exceed the industry average by nearly 50%, while this past year's revenue growth of 24% blew away the industry average of 1.7%.

Scoring Guidant is a little tricky because of its experience with EVA. My inclination is to give the company credit in the leadership, strategic planning, information and analysis, process management, and organizational performance areas because EVA is so systemic. Whereas Dana was fairly new to the concept, Guidant's five-year effort suggests broad integration and deployment. I gave Guidant 40 points for EVA, distributed as shown in the following chart.

Domini recognition scored 4 points in 1.2. The ISO certification earns 8 points for process management (6.1) and 8 points for organizational performance (7.5). Being designated as one of the Best Companies to Work For suggests motivated and satisfied employees, earning it 8 for 5.2, and its training hours per employee bring it 4 points for 5.1 and 8 for 7.3. Guidant's exceptional financial performance deserves 16 points for 7.2.

With a total of 92 points, Guidant makes my cut as a well-managed company.

Guidant Corporation Management Screen

IQ	*Area*	*Score*
Senior leader involvement (EVA)	1.1	4
Corporate responsibility (Domini)	1.2	4
Strategy deployment (EVA)	2.2	4
EVA—measurement	4.1	8
EVA—analysis	4.2	8
Training	5.1	4
Satisfied employees: Best Companies to Work For	5.2	8
Process management: ISO and EVA	6.1	12
Financial performance	7.2	16
Human resources performance (training)	7.3	8
Organizational performance	7.5	16
	Total:	92

Johnson Controls (JCI)

I first came across Johnson Controls in *Industry Week*'s list of Best Plants in America for 1999, then noticed the name again when a Johnson Controls purchasing circle surfaced on Amazon.com under a Six Sigma book.

Fortune magazine lumps Johnson Controls in the Motor Vehicles and Parts category, where it was the fifth-ranked company in the magazine's most recent Most Admired list—behind four automobile manufacturers. The company also manufactures and installs control systems for nonresidential buildings and manages facilities for commercial and government buildings worldwide.

Johnson Controls obviously values process thinking. Six of its plants have won the Shingo Prize—more than any other company can claim—and nearly 50 of its facilities are ISO certified. One group, the Patuxent River BOS Project, earned a Silver Maryland Quality Award in both 1997 and 1998.

The company's process focus extends to its suppliers. Best Practices, LLC recognized Johnson Controls for supply chain management. *Information Week* honored the company as a top technology innovator.

Johnson Controls also values employee training. A presentation at ASQ's 1995 annual conference described how "workers are in charge of their own learning process" using Johnson Control's competency-based training program. An abstract of the presentation I found at ASQ's Web site noted that, "after a one-day training session, workers demonstrated an increase of knowledge of 39 to 67 percent."

The company's revenue growth surpasses the industry average going back ten years, while its return on equity, return on assets, and return on invested capital for the past five years are average.

Process management, evident in the Shingo Prizes, ISO-certified plants, Maryland Quality Awards, and Best Plants recognition, earns Johnson Controls 12 points for 6.1 and 16 points for 7.5. Supply chain management deserves 4 points for 6.2 and 8 points for 7.4. Being honored as a technology innovator serves as a proxy for evidence of a performance measurement system, earning 8 points for 4.1. The training program receives 4 points for 5.1 and 4 points for 7.3, while Johnson Controls' financial performance and its Most Admired status warrant 12 points for 7.2.

This is one case where the total score of 68 isn't as high as my impression of the company. Any company with such extensive ISO certification and recognition through Shingo Prizes and a state quality award program obviously understands and is improving its management system. Rather than mess with my interpretation of the Management Screen and arbitrarily assign points to other categories, I'd choose to use the score as a guideline and follow up with further research and a phone call to the company to verify the quality of its management system.

Johnson Controls Management Screen

IQ	*Area*	*Score*
Technology innovation	4.1	8
Training program	5.1	4
Process management: Shingo, ISO, MD Quality Awards	6.1	12
Supply chain management	6.2	4
Financial performance	7.2	12
Human resource performance	7.3	4
Supplier performance	7.4	8
Organizational performance	7.5	16
	Total:	68

Manitowoc Company (MTW)

Manitowoc makes commercial ice machines, ice and beverage dispensers, and other refrigeration products, manufactures cranes, and builds and fixes ships. I'd never heard of the company until it appeared on Stern Stewart's EVA site.

According to the company's 1999 annual report, which I tracked down using 10K Wizard, Manitowoc has been using EVA since 1993. The same report mentions that the company is pursuing ISO certification; *Quality Digest*'s ISO database confirms that it's now ISO certified. I couldn't find any other information about Manitowoc running the same searches I did for the other companies in this chapter.

Manitowoc's financial indicators are at or above the industry average for the past five years, with the exception of revenue growth, which far surpassed the industry. Manitowoc's revenue grew 15.9% over the past year compared with the industry average of a negative 2.5%, and over five years its revenue grew at 43.2% compared to the average of 5.6%.

As with Guidant, I gave Manitowoc broad credit for its lengthy experience with EVA: 4 points in the leadership area, 4 points in strategy deployment, 16 points in information and analysis, 4 points in process management, and 8 points in organizational performance.

ISO certification adds another 8 points for process management and 8 points for organizational performance. I also awarded Manitowoc 12 points for its financial performance, for a total of 64 points. I would want to learn more about Manitowoc's management system and competitive environment, but it certainly appears to be a well-managed company.

Manitowoc Corporation Management Screen

IQ	*Area*	*Score*
Senior leader involvement (EVA)	1.1	4
Strategy deployment (EVA)	2.2	4
EVA—measurement	4.1	8
EVA—analysis	4.2	8
Process management: ISO and EVA	6.1	12
Financial performance	7.2	12
Organizational performance	7.5	16
	Total:	64

Marriott International (MAR)

Ritz-Carlton Hotel Company is the only service company to win the Baldrige Award twice. Its merger with Marriott in 1997 left me wondering if the cultures were compatible, or if Ritz-Carlton was an island of quality in an indifferent system.

I learned that, while the quality of Ritz-Carlton's management system may be more advanced, the system fits well with Marriott's agenda. According to *Fortune*, Marriott ranked first in the Hotels, Casinos, and Resorts category on its 1999 Most Admired List and was also a member of the Best Companies to Work For list (which shows 40 hours training per employee per year). APQC recognized Marriott for its new product development process and featured the company in a book on empowerment, an area validated by Best

Practices, LLC, which honored Marriott for employee performance management. Best Practices also listed Marriott for its benchmarking acumen. Domini included it in its Social Index.

The company appears to be committed to employee satisfaction. It appeared on *Business Week*'s list of family-friendly companies. A search of Amazon.com revealed a 1998 book by J.W. Marriott Jr. called *The Spirit to Serve: The Marriott Way*, in which the company's chairman and CEO talks about motivating employees and developing loyal customers.

Marriott is one of two companies I researched for this chapter (Whirlpool is the other) that participates in the American Customer Satisfaction Index (ACSI). Its scores since 1994 have been steady at around 77, compared with the industry average of 72.

Based on the numbers I got off Quicken.com, its financial performance ranks slightly above average. Return on equity (ROE) for the past five years was below the industry average (7.6% compared with 10.6), while return on assets (ROA) and return on invested capital (ROIC) were average. Marriott's revenue grew 9.7% over the past year compared with the industry average of negative 0.02%.

To score the company, I started with a baseline 40 points for its two-time Baldrige Award–winning subsidiary. Making the Most Admired list, combined with its generally positive financial indicators, earned it 6 points for 7.2.

Marriott's presence on the Best Companies to Work For list and family-friendly list, together with the CEO's emphasis on employees in his book, added up to 8 points for 5.2. Its recognition for employee empowerment and performance management and its training hours per employee earned 10 points for 5.1 and 8 points in 7.3. The fact that the CEO wrote a book focused on motivating employees and retaining customers warrants 8 points in 1.1, while its presence in the Domini Social Index earned it 4 points for 1.2.

Best practices in new product development and benchmarking

deserve 4 points each (6.1 and 4.1). Marriott's participation in the ACSI and its drive to create loyal customers earn the company 8 points for 3.1 and 2 points for 3.2. ACSI scores above the industry average count for 10 points in 7.1.

With its two Baldrige Awards, Ritz-Carlton exemplifies quality management in a service organization. With its many indicators of quality, Marriott International deservedly ranks as a well-managed company.

Marriott International Management Screen

IQ	*Area*	*Score*
Baldrige Awards: Ritz-Carlton	All	40
Senior leader involvement	1.1	8
Corporate responsibility (Domini)	1.2	4
Customer focus and new product development	3.1	8
Commitment to customer loyalty	3.2	2
Benchmarking	4.1	4
Employee empowerment, performance management, training	5.1	10
Employee satisfaction and motivation (Most Admired)	5.2	8
New product development	6.1	4
Customer satisfaction performance	7.1	10
Financial performance	7.2	6
Human resources performance	7.3	8
	Total:	112

MBNA Corporation (KRB)

Like Marriott, MBNA promotes a strong customer focus. MBNA is an independent credit card lender and leading issuer of affinity credit cards. While it's one of those companies that tends to show up repeatedly in discussions of quality management, I noticed MBNA in a *Harvard Business Review* article that described how executives listen in on customer service phone calls. A quick trip to the SEC filings found this quote in the company's 1998 annual report: "On average, MBNA customers carry balances that are 45 percent higher than the industry average. [Our] focus is on the quality of each customer." Best Practices, LLC acknowledges MBNA's efforts in this area by recognizing its customer satisfaction practices.

In my experience, the companies that excel at customer satisfaction also lead the way in employee satisfaction, and MBNA proves the point. It ranked first on *Business Week*'s family-friendly list and tenth on *Fortune*'s 1999 Best Companies to Work For list. According to *Business Week*, 78% of MBNA's employees said that family issues didn't hurt their career progress.

The sense of community that encompasses customers and employees extends to MBNA's communities. The MBNA Education Foundation provides financial support for improving the quality and availability of education in its communities. MBNA is also part of the Domini Social Index.

MBNA's return on assets and invested capital are double the industry average for the past five years, while return on equity at 29.8% far exceeds the average of 18.9%. Revenue grew 24.9% over the past year compared with the industry average of 3.6%. MBNA also ranked second in the Consumer Credit category on *Fortune*'s Most Admired list.

I gave MBNA 28 points for its customer focus, 12 for 3.1, 4 for 3.2, and 12 for 7.1. Its employee focus earned the company 8 points for 5.2 and 8 points for 7.3, while the MBNA Education Foundation and Domini presence added 8 points in 1.2. The company's stellar financial performance combined with its Most Admired status contributed 16 points to 7.2, for a total of 68 points.

What's obvious about these results is that my findings related only to a small portion of the Management Screen. I would have liked to find some evidence of process management or a measurement system, both of which are areas I would research further.

MBNA Corporation Management Screen

IQ	*Area*	*Score*
Community involvement (Ed. Foundation & Domini)	1.2	8
Customer focus	3.1	12
Customer satisfaction/loyalty	3.2	4
Employee satisfaction	5.2	8
Customer satisfaction performance	7.1	12
Financial performance	7.2	16
Human resource performance	7.3	8
	Total:	68

Rohm & Haas (ROH)

Rohm & Haas appeared as a purchasing circle on Amazon.com for a book I originally found on General Electric's purchasing circle list. A review of SEC filings explains why: Rohm & Haas received a Six Sigma Quality Award from GE in 1998.

Rohm & Haas is a chemical and plastics manufacturer. Aside from the award reference in its annual report, the only other mention of the company came in *Quality Digest*'s ISO database, which listed more than a dozen ISO-certified facilities.

The company's financial performance is average except for revenue growth. Its ROE, ROA, and ROIC are all around the industry average. Revenue growth has exceeded the average for the past three-, five-, and ten-year periods, with 43.5% growth in the past year compared with the industry average of 0.08%.

All of this leaves not much information to produce a score. The Six Sigma Quality Award doesn't necessarily mean Rohm & Haas has implemented Six Sigma, but it does mean the company has achieved high levels of quality that probably aren't possible without a good understanding of customer requirements, a solid measurement system, process management and improvement, and improving performance on key measures. That, together with its ISO-certified facilities, earns Rohm & Haas 12 points for satisfying customer requirements (3.1), 4 points for its measurement system (4.1), 12 points for process management (6.1), 8 points for customer satisfaction performance (7.1), and 12 points for organizational performance (7.5). I also gave the company 6 points for financial performance for a total of 54 points. I'd like to know more about that Six Sigma Award before deciding whether the company truly is well managed.

Rohm & Haas Management Screen

IQ	*Area*	*Score*
Satisfying customer requirements	3.1	12
Measurement system	4.1	4
Process management (ISO)	6.1	12
Customer satisfaction performance	7.1	8
Financial performance	7.2	6
Organizational performance	7.5	12
	Total:	54

SPX Corporation (SPW)

SPX manufactures components for automotive, industrial, and technology customers. It showed up on radar when Stern Stewart listed it as an EVA client. Its annual report confirms the implementation of EVA as far back as 1997. In its 1998 annual report, SPX describes its Value Improvement Process, which includes EVA as well as deploying leadership standards throughout the company and completing a strategic review process.

A dozen SPX facilities have been ISO certified. The company has also been recognized by *Industry Week* for having a Best Plant. SPX is part of the Domini Social Index.

The company's financial performance runs hot and cold. Its revenue has grown 40% per year over the past three years compared with the industry average of 10.5%, but it is far below the industry average for the past three years in return on equity, return on assets, and return on invested capital.

Using the same guidelines for EVA that I applied to Guidant, I gave it 40 points as shown in the following chart. The deployment of leadership standards deserves 4 points in 1.1, inclusion in the Domini index earns 4 points in 1.2, and the mention of a strategic review process earns 8 points in 2.1. ISO certification and Best Plant honors score 8 points in 6.1 and 8 points for organizational performance. I added another 4 points for financial performance, for a total of 68 points, which is certainly enough to warrant a second look.

SPX Corporation Management Screen

IQ	*Area*	*Score*
Senior leader involvement (EVA and leadership standards)	1.1	8
Corporate responsibility (Domini)	1.2	4
Strategy deployment (EVA and strategic review process)	2.2	8
EVA—measurement	4.1	8
EVA—analysis	4.2	8
Process management: ISO and EVA	6.1	12
Financial performance	7.2	4
Organizational performance	7.5	16
	Total:	68

Staples Inc. (SPLS)

Staples has more than 900 office products superstores in the United States, Canada, the United Kingdom, and Germany (and not a one in Minnesota). In *Total Quality Management,* I described how the company learns from and serves its customers, but that was the extent of my probing into its management system.

I found nothing of value about Staples in its annual report, nor did I fare any better with ASQ, APQC, EVA, or ISO. Staples did make *Information Week*'s list for technology innovation, and Best Practices, LLC recognized it for its call center. It is also part of the Domini Social Index. That's it.

Staples excelled in financial performance. Return on equity, return on assets, and return on invested capital for the last five years were all well above the industry average. Its revenue grew 24.1% over the past year compared with the industry average of 1.75%.

This one's pretty easy to add up. I'd give it 4 points for Domini (1.2), 12 points for satisfying customers (3.1), 4 points for building customer relationships (4), 8 points for technology innovation (4.1), 8 points for customer satisfaction performance (7.1), and 16 points for financial performance (7.2), for a total of 52 points. That's not a very impressive score for such a large company, but it may suggest hidden indicators of quality management that more research could uncover. Until that information was found, however, I'd reserve judgment.

Staples Inc. Management Screen

IQ	*Area*	*Score*
Corporate responsibility (Domini)	1.2	4
Satisfying customer requirements	3.1	12
Building customer relationships	3.2	4
Measurement system (technology innovation)	4.1	8
Customer satisfaction performance	7.1	8
Financial performance	7.2	16
	Total:	52

Starbucks Corporation (SBUX)

Starbucks appeared on Best Practices, LLC's study of high-performance teams along with well-managed and well-known peers Motorola, Hewlett-Packard, Eaton, and Microsoft. Its inclusion in this exemplary group intrigued me, so I decided to screen it.

I returned to the Best Practices Web site and found Starbucks recognized for employee performance management and development. APQC identified it for best practices in three areas: supplier partnerships, involving customers and suppliers in the design process, and using customer information. In this last area, APQC noted that Starbucks "tries to make everyone in the company more aware and accountable to the customer." It does this by forwarding relevant customer comments and information to district and store managers for further action.

Fortune magazine named it one of the Best Companies to Work For, noting that all employees are called partners, and they all get stock options. Starbucks is also part of the Domini Social Index.

Starbucks' financial performance is impressive. Its return on equity of 9.5% for the past five years compares with a negative 6.9% for the Specialty Eateries industry, with ROA and ROIC showing similar results. Its revenue grew 29.9% in the past year versus the industry average of 18.4%.

Starbucks' recognition for best practices in two areas related to employee performance, along with its liberal stock option program for all employees, deserves 12 points in 5.1. Making the Best Companies to Work For list adds 8 points in 5.2 and the Domini index another 4 points in 1.2. The company's strong employee focus warrants 8 points in 7.3. Involving customers and suppliers in the design process and using customer information earns 8 points in 3.1, 8 points in 3.2, 8 points in 6.1, and 8 points in 7.1. The supplier involvement gets a nod with 4 points in 6.2. Starbucks' strong financial performance scores 16 points in 7.2.

With a total of 84 points and in light of its industry's poor financial results, I'd consider Starbucks a well-managed company.

Starbucks Corporation Management Screen

IQ	*Area*	*Score*
Corporate responsibility (Domini)	1.2	4
Using customer information	3.1	8
Using customer information and call center excellence	3.2	8
Employee performance mgmt., stock options	5.1	12
Employee satisfaction (Most Admired)	5.2	8
Customers/supplier involvement in design process	6.1	8
Supplier involvement	6.2	4
Customer satisfaction performance	7.1	8
Financial performance	7.2	16
Human resources performance	7.3	8
	Total:	84

Whirlpool Corporation (WHR)

I didn't expect an old-time manufacturer of home appliances to be featured in the trendy *Fast Company*, so when I read about Whirlpool's Real Whirled training program, I decided to check out the company's management system.

The first quality indicator I discovered involved Whirlpool's measurement system. It has implemented EVA according to Stern Stewart's EVA Web site. At APQC's site, it earned recognition for its advanced measurement system based on four Value Creating Objectives: customer satisfaction, total quality, people commitment, and growth and innovation. The measurement system reflects a Balanced Scorecard.

APQC also identified Whirlpool for best practices in the area of strategic planning, while Best Practices, LLC listed it for executive communication. As a participant in the American Customer Satisfaction Index, Whirlpool has maintained steady scores since 1994 that are slightly above the industry average. It's also in the Domini Social Index.

Whirlpool's financial performance outpaced the industry average, most notably in return on invested capital over a five-year period (4.5% for Whirlpool compared with 2.9% average) and return on equity (6.9% compared with 5.1%). Revenue growth also exceeded the industry average as far back as ten years. *Fortune* named Whirlpool to its Most Admired Companies list in 1999.

Let's add it up. EVA and the Value Creating Objectives earn Whirlpool 10 points for its measurement system (4.1) and 10 points for measurement analysis (4.2). EVA combined with best practices in executive communication count for 8 points in 1.1. Domini presence means 4 points in 1.2. The company's four objectives and best practices in strategic planning add 8 points for 2.1 and 8 points for 2.2. Participation in the ACSI surveys and an objective focused on customer satisfaction score 12 points for 3.1 and 8 points for 7.1. Its presence on the Most Admired list along with above-average financial performance earned Whirlpool 12 points in 7.2, for a grand total of 76 points.

What's odd about Whirlpool's score is that it earned points in every category except the two most common categories in my random survey: human resources and process management. With any evidence of quality performance in either area, I'd consider Whirlpool a well-managed company.

Whirlpool Corporation Management Screen

IQ	*Area*	*Score*
Executive communication	1.1	8
Corporate responsibility (Domini)	1.2	4
Strategic planning process	2.1	8
Strategic plan deployment	2.2	8
Satisfying customer requirements	3.1	12
Measurement system (EVA and Value Creating Objectives)	4.1	10
Measurement analysis (EVA/Value Creating Objectives)	4.2	10
Customer satisfaction performance	7.1	8
Financial performance	7.2	12
	Total:	76

Yahoo! Inc. (YHOO)

I like Yahoo!, both as a search engine and as a place to pick up a card game or two. When deciding which Internet stock to include in the chapter, I started with a couple of smaller companies to see what I could find. There was nothing. They're just too young and too focused on generating growth to communicate anything about their management systems. So I turned to Yahoo!

A search of SEC filings turned up annual reports but no hits on quality, EPA, or any other IQs. I tried "growth" and got a plethora of information, including an explanation in the 1998 annual report that "Yahoo! must continue to implement and improve its operational and 18 financial systems and to expand, train, and manage its employee base." Beyond that, the annual report reflected the business media's coverage of the company: heavy on uncontrollable Internet factors, mergers and acquisitions, and warnings about earnings.

I then searched the same sites I used for the other companies and came up with one piece of management-related information. Best Practices, LLC included Yahoo! in a book about the use of financial performance measures. The reference likely relates to the company's 18 financial systems.

Those financial systems may help explain why Yahoo! is outperforming the industry in ROE, ROA, ROIC, and revenue growth.

That's not much to go on when evaluating a management system, and the score reflects it. I find it heartening that Yahoo! devoted annual report space to comments about improving its operational system and training its employees. A discussion with investor relations about those and other points may confirm that this is a well-managed company—especially in such a dynamic industry.

Yahoo! Inc. Management Screen

IQ	*Area*	*Score*
Financial measurement system	2.1	4
Financial measurement analysis	4.2	4
Financial performance	7.2	16
	Total:	24

Who Makes the Cut

My random sample (emphasis on random) of 16 companies produced a Management Screen scoring range of 24 to 116 points. For this list, my arbitrary cutoff point for consideration as a well-managed company turned out to be 84, putting five companies in that elite group. With a little more supporting information, most likely attainable with a phone call to the company, I'm confident the next six would make the cut as well. The last five, all scoring less than 55 points, would require significantly more evidence for me to be able to evaluate the quality of their management systems.

Quality Scores

Company	*Score*	*Market Cap (mil.) (3/1/2000)*	*Industry*
Dana	116	$ 3,608	Auto Parts
Eaton	116	$ 5,534	Auto Parts
Marriott International	112	$ 6,664	Lodging
Guidant	92	$22,150	Medical Instruments/Supplies
Starbucks	84	$ 6,378	Specialty Eateries
Whirlpool	76	$ 3,926	Appliances
SPX	68	$ 3,383	Auto Parts
MBNA	68	$18,491	Credit Services
Johnson Controls	68	$ 4,454	Auto Parts
CIGNA	66	$13,156	Property/Casualty Insurance
Manitowoc	64	$ 684	Farm/Construction Machinery
Rohm & Haas	54	$ 8,263	Chemicals—Major Diversified
Staples	52	$10,165	Specialty Retail, Other
Black Box	38	$ 1,417	Networking & Comm. Devices
Ceridian	34	$ 2,875	Business Software & Services
Yahoo!	24	$83,183	Internet Information Providers

You'll notice in the list of companies that market capitalization size doesn't impede the assessment of managerial competence. The only small-cap stock, Manitowoc, scored well. Two mid-cap stocks ended up near the bottom of the list, but both scored better than the market-cap giant, Yahoo! "Dot coms" are the next quality frontier, as yet providing little evidence of systematic performance improvement.

I found it harder to locate information about smaller companies because most of the business buzz surrounds bigger and better-known companies, but the information's not impossible to find. On the positive side, a phone call to investor relations at a small-cap company is more likely to produce fruitful results than one to a large-cap behemoth.

You'll also notice that, while type of industry had an impact, it didn't shape the list. The automotive industry is known for high-quality standards, so it wasn't surprising to find the four auto parts companies scoring well.

Finally, all these companies except Yahoo! made my list because they appeared in some sort of quality context in a magazine article, Web site, or book. The source predisposed the companies to display some quality management behaviors. You're less likely to get these levels of Management Screen scores if the companies you're screening have no quality bias to begin with.

Chapter 8

What to Do with What You Learn

If you're a quality engineer, screening companies to assess management system quality may pass as high entertainment. What could be more rewarding than recognizing a quality practitioner for years of thankless improvements, or putting a poor-scoring quality skeptic in its place?

Investors, on the other hand, only endure management screening if it promises to improve the return on their investments. Sure, finding out how a company fares with the Management Screen is interesting, but unless the exercise contributes to better decisions, it's wasted time. You can know that management quality matters. You can have a good idea of what management quality is. You can even evaluate management quality at a potential investment. But if you're not sure what to do with what you learn, the process is pointless.

Before we can get to what's next, we need to discuss risk and value and how they relate to a well-managed company. No matter what their investment strategies, investors want to buy stocks that will minimize the risk as they grow in value. Well-managed companies work both sides of that street.

Minimizing Risk while Increasing Value

Stock prices tend to make their biggest moves because of changes in macroeconomic factors: fears of inflation or recession; rising or declining interest rates; changes in government policies; economic cycles; business trends. These issues account for great swings in the value of individual stocks and end up dominating stock market discussions, as seen nightly on CNN's *Moneyline* television show, which spends most of its time debating the impact of Alan Greenspan's latest speech, the longevity of the bull market, and the growing impact of technology stocks.

The Management Screen has little to do with these macroeconomic factors. As part of a company's strategic planning process, one would hope it considers economic, governmental, and industry changes. Such consideration would qualify it for a few extra points in the Strategic Planning area, but that's about the extent of it. Instead, the focus of the Management Screen, and of a management system, is on the microeconomic factors that help shape a company's success and, as a result, its exposure to risk.

These microeconomic factors are management quality, product and service quality, innovation, revenue, and costs. The only one of these factors that's plainly visible to investors is revenue. To evaluate the rest of the factors you need to look at a company slightly differently, like those "magic" pictures that were a fad a few years ago, where you crossed your eyes or blurred your vision and suddenly a different image appeared. The common way of evaluating management doesn't work here. You need the "magic" vision of the Management Screen.

The screen encompasses all the elements of management quality. It evaluates product and service quality by looking at what customers require (3.1), how products and services are designed, produced, and delivered (6.1), how well a company does this (7.5), and how satisfied customers are with the result (3.2 and 7.1). It assesses innovation in 1.1, 3.1, 5.1, and 6.1. It considers cost control throughout the management system by focusing on improvements in quality and speed and reductions in waste and costs.

A management system can create value two ways: increasing revenues and reducing costs. A company increases revenues by building the ranks of loyal customers through high-quality products and services, competitive prices, and exceptional service. It cuts costs by continually improving its processes to reduce waste and increase productivity. While information about a company's revenues is readily available, information about cost control remains hidden unless a company reports it, as Honeywell did in its 1998 annual report: "Honeywell's net income increased 21 percent in 1998, primarily due to the benefits of Honeywell Quality Value (HQV) Operational Excellence, focused on reducing costs. Net income was $572 million in 1998, compared with $471 million in 1997 and $403 million in 1996." Chapter 2 shows the correlation between HQV, icreasing revenues, and reducing costs, providing a real-world example of how improvements in both sides of the equation increase shareholder value (Figure 8.1).

The improvements made to create and maintain a quality management system also help reduce risk for investors. Consider the microeconomic factors again:

- Product and service quality are defined by customers. A company that knows exactly what its customers require and how well it is meeting those requirements is likely to be less risky

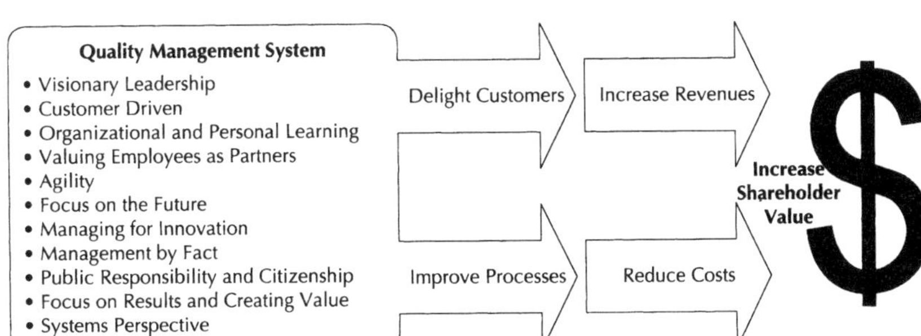

Figure 8.1 **Increasing Shareholder Value**

than a company that thinks it knows what its customers want and hopes they're buying it.

- Innovation is a function of empowering and training people and turning them loose on products, services, and processes. A company that nurtures teams, encourages creativity, and promotes training is likely to be less risky than a hierarchical, command-and-control company that inhibits thinking.
- Cost control is a natural byproduct of quality management. Just listen to Jack Welch boast about how much GE is saving through Six Sigma. A company that relentlessly pursues improvement is likely to be less risky than a company that must spend all its energy putting out fires.
- Management quality is measured by the Management Screen. A company that scores well is likely to be less risky than a company that does not.

Benjamin Graham concurred, noting in *The Intelligent Investor* that "good management produces a good average market price, and bad management produces bad market prices." Screening a company's management system helps reduce the risk of investing in a badly managed company.

Good management also makes the stock more predictable. Take another look at Solectron's stock performance (Figure 1.1 in Chapter 1). It doesn't get much more predictable than that.

But that's an electronics company, you say, and they're known for quality management. What about a service company in an industry rarely mentioned in quality circles?

Consider Starbucks. As Figure 8.2 illustrates, this specialty eatery's stock performance has also been predictable. Sure it's had its peaks and valleys, but the value of the stock continues to climb.

Good management also produces more positive surprises. Despite analysts' best attempts to keep all surprises to a minimum, fine-tuning their estimates of earnings per share to the penny, companies still exceed or fall short of the projections. A quality management system increases the likelihood of more positive than negative surprises.

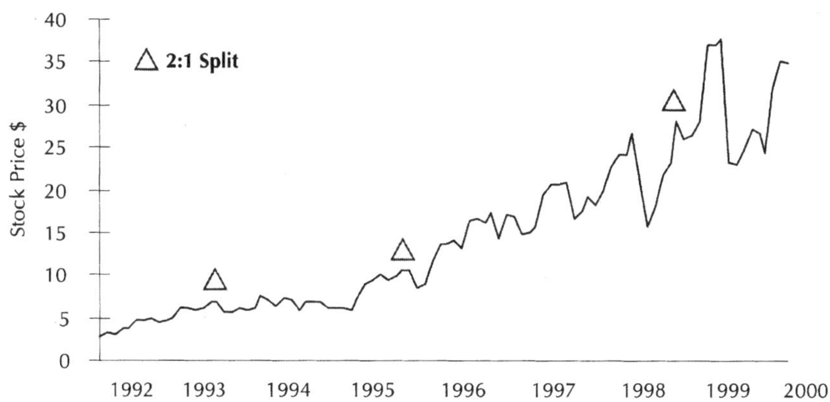

Figure 8.2 **Starbucks Corporation's Stock Performance**

A Screen for All Strategies

No matter what investment strategy you employ, it will be better with the addition of a management screen. If you're a value investor and you come across a low price-to-earnings gem, before you light that candle, run the Management Screen. A strong score may reassure you that the company is indeed a great value, while a poor score may indicate that the good value is really a dog.

If you're a growth investor and you spot rapidly growing revenues and an amazing return on equity, before you buy, invoke the Management Screen. A high score may tell you that the revenues will continue to climb, while a low score may warn you about unsustainable growth.

The Management Screen also works with a diversified portfolio. As we saw in the previous chapter, almost any type of company can be evaluated with the possible exception of Internet stocks or very young companies. Screening the management systems of several companies in an industry gives you another way to differentiate them beyond just financial performance and analysts' recommendations.

In fact, screening several companies in an industry is an excellent way to find out what passes as quality management in that industry. The scores for companies in the auto parts industry, as shown in the previous chapter, tend to be high, as will scores for electronics companies, while the scores for service and technology companies tend to be lower. My scoring in the previous chapter put Ceridian at 34 points and Dana at 115 and both are in the Q-100. Whatever the range, the higher-scoring companies in an industry will tend to outperform the lower-scoring ones over time.

Proof of the performance of well-managed companies can be found in the Q-100, a diversified portfolio that includes value and growth stocks, and in the Hendricks-Singhal study presented in the first chapter. Taking no other factor into consideration than the quality of their management systems, the stock of companies in the Q-100 perform better than the S&P 500 as a whole. And that's the key to profiting from well-managed companies.

Underappreciated and Undervalued

Well-managed companies are better investments than those who don't qualify for the title. Here's the logic behind that statement:

- Well-managed companies outperform those companies with average or worse management, increasing revenues and reducing costs to improve shareholder value.
- Wall Street does not yet recognize the fact that well-managed companies have greater value than their counterparts.
- The difference between what well-managed companies are worth and what Wall Street thinks they are worth is your chance to profit from well-managed companies, because the quality of their management systems will pull up their stock prices as perceived value catches up to actual value.

Honeywell's performance from 1994 to 1998 illustrates the lag time between what analysts think a stock is worth and its actual value. Recall from Chapter 2 that Honeywell began conducting internal assessments of its management system in 1994 through a process called the Honeywell Quality Value (HQV). From 1993 to 1995 the price of a share of Honeywell stock barely moved, but then it began to climb (Figure 8.3). A correlation among HQV scores, earnings per share, and stock price shows that it took analysts *two years* to recognize the value of an improving management system.

Your opportunity lasts as long as a gap exists between what analysts think a stock is worth and what it's actually worth based on the company's performance. Analysts tend to think of management in macroeconomic terms. One mutual fund manager described superior management as management "that knows how to get rid of businesses that aren't good, knows how to acquire wisely, and if they don't, knows how to get the capital back to shareholders." That's a pretty common definition. The Management Screen offers a different definition with proven results. Since few analysts have learned how to assess the quality of a management system and even fewer believe (at this time) that it matters all that much, the gap remains—for now.

Peter Lynch calls this an asset play, meaning "any company that's sitting on something valuable that you know about, but that

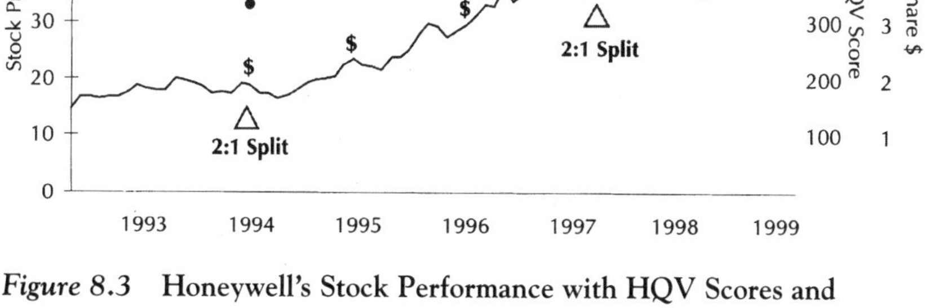

Figure 8.3 Honeywell's Stock Performance with HQV Scores and Earnings per Share

the Wall Street crowd has overlooked" (*One Up on Wall Street*, Penguin Books, 1990). Companies with quality management systems are definitely sitting on something valuable. With a little research, you'll know enough about it to recognize its value. And you're probably safe in thinking that Wall Street will overlook it, since there's nothing particularly dramatic or intriguing about a management system.

The business media pay little attention to the subject because the only time it's considered newsworthy is when a much-publicized senior executive like Jack Welch talks about saving billions through Six Sigma. Otherwise, the headlines go to the CEO's next big plan or purchase or failure. It's what business and investment analysts want to read. What analyst is going to impress his or her colleagues with tales of Balanced Scorecards or EVA when they've got mergers and acquisitions and Alan Greenspan's last/next speech to debate?

This management system stuff isn't glamorous, and as long as it remains that way, you've got an asset play on any company intent on improving the quality of its management system.

How to Profit from Well-Managed Companies

Invest in them.

Not to be too simplistic, but once you've run the Management Screen and determined that, in your judgment, a company has a quality management system, and after you've done your financial analysis and found that the company fits your investment and diversification strategy, you can invest in the company any time you want. It's hard enough to try to time the market based on financial or macroeconomic factors, but it's impossible to time a management system. A company is systematically improving it or it's not. At a certain level of improvement, a level you decide using the Management Screen, that improvement helps drive the company's stock performance, as Honeywell's experience shows.

The problem is that not many companies meet the criteria for well-managed status. And by the time they do, gains in their stock price may already have obviated the value of the Management Screen.

What's needed, then, is a process for identifying well-managed or soon-to-be well-managed companies before they appear on analysts' radar screens. I propose two approaches.

Well-Managed and Ready to Roll

The first approach is to run the Management Screen on companies you've identified to see if they cross the well-managed threshold. If they do, if they're close, or if much of their IQs are recent, check their stock price to see if it reflects improvements in the management system. If the stock price is declining, more research is needed to see what is causing the decline. If the stock performance is flat or rising slightly, you may have found an investment opportunity.

Johnson Controls provides one example. As noted in the previous chapter, Johnson Controls is one of *Fortune* magazine's Most Admired companies in the Motor Vehicles and Parts category (the top-ranked company in the "Parts" piece of that sector). The company's stock performance since 1994 is shown in Figure 8.4. I picked 1994 because it was probably the first year Johnson Controls would have appeared in an investor's search for indicators of quality: A few of its plants earned ISO certification that year.

In 1995, Johnson Controls explained its competency-based training program to attendees at the American Society for Quality's annual conference. The company's stock price began to recover from a late-year slump.

If you had been screening management systems back then, Johnson Controls would have popped up in your searches in 1994 and again in 1995, but it probably wouldn't have scored too well on the screen until 1996. That year, most of the company's facilities achieved ISO certification and two plants won the Shingo Prize. Revenues and earnings per share grew 20% over the previous year.

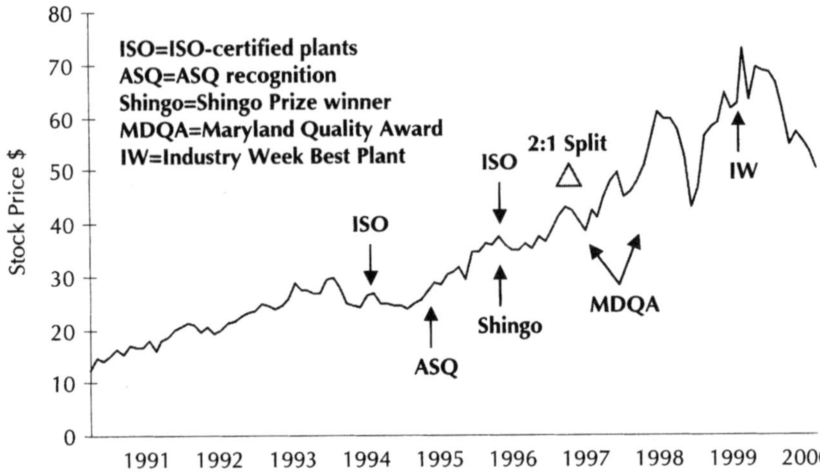

Figure 8.4 Johnson Controls' Stock Performance with IQ Milestones

If you had invested in Johnson Controls at the end of 1996, which was the first time it would have been likely to enter the well-managed realm, your stock would have nearly doubled in value by early 1999 before falling back as the year progressed. Hey, no company, no matter how good its management system, is immune to the vagaries of the economy, its industry, or other macroeconomic factors.

At the same time, after you've looked at a number of stock trends for well-managed companies, you'll notice a similar strong incline in their performance. That incline may be interrupted by a factor beyond the purview of a management system, but that's usually not the system's fault.

All of this assumes investing in the stock based on the quality of its management system without thought to financial analysis—which means I'm doing this for demonstration purposes only. You'll want to look at as much of the picture as you can, including managerial competence and financial performance and prospects, before making an investment decision.

SPX Corporation provides an even more dramatic example. Like Johnson Controls, it would have appeared in your IQ searches early with an *Industry Week* Best Plant in 1991 and an ISO-certified plant (the same one, it turns out) in 1993. Neither event seemed to affect stock performance (Figure 8.5).

About a dozen more plants became ISO-certified in 1996, at which point the stock took off. Like Johnson Controls, SPX has stuttered in the last couple years, but such normal variation doesn't diminish the fact that its stock was worth five times more in January 2000 than it was four years earlier.

"That's fine," you're probably thinking, "if I'm looking to invest in manufacturing companies, but what if I'm not?" To be honest, the onset of quality management is harder to detect at service companies than manufacturing companies, and it's almost impossible to find in technology stocks. That limits your options, but it doesn't remove them.

I thought about using Ceridian or Staples as an example, but since I hadn't found any major IQs for either earlier than Ceridian's 1999 annual report, I couldn't demonstrate possible cause-

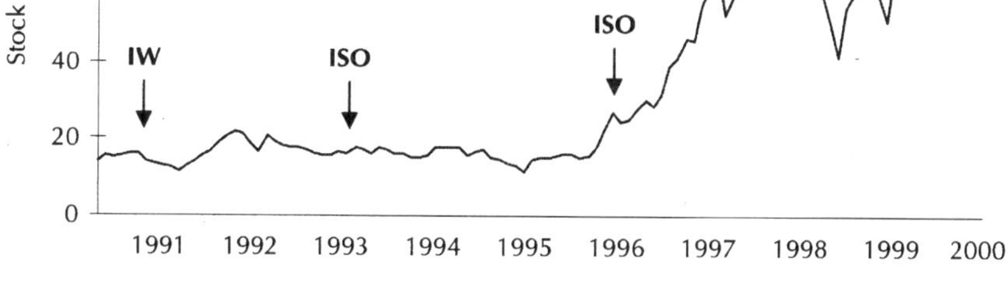

Figure 8.5 SPX Corporation's Stock Performance with IQ Milestones

and-effect. Instead I took another service company from Chapter 7: Starbucks.

By my searches, Starbucks would have first appeared in 1996 when APQC used it as one example of how to use customer information. Two years later, APQC again used Starbucks as a role model, this time for supplier partnerships and involving customers and suppliers in its design process.

That's not much to go on, although being featured for best practices in three different areas is certainly admirable. If you look at Starbucks' stock performance (Figure 8.6), the beginning of its strongest ascent can be traced to 1996, but I'm not sure an investor would have trusted one mention in ASQC as evidence of quality management. If, however, an investor had felt confident that three best practices (and strong financial performance) qualified as evidence and invested in Starbucks in 1998, he or she would still have realized a 50% gain by March 2000.

The first approach to investing in well-managed companies relies on waiting until a company can score enough points on the Management Screen to verify the quality of its management system. The second approach, while riskier, offers more opportunity for investment gains.

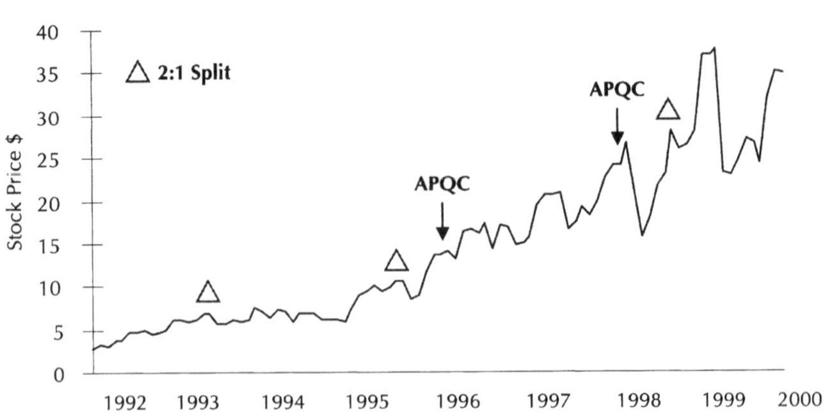

Figure 8.6 **Starbucks' Stock Performance with IQ Milestones**

Ready to Become Well-Managed

The second approach to investing in well-managed companies is to find them before they've established the quality of their management systems. In Starbucks' case, that would have been in 1996 when the first evidence of any management system expertise appeared. For SPX it would have been in 1991, while Johnson Controls would have surfaced in 1994.

Investing in a company before it has a quality management system in place exposes investors to the risk that the indicator of quality is a fluke, an orphan quality moment in an otherwise sterile management system. For every Starbucks, SPX, or Johnson Controls, there is a company that tried quality on and didn't like the fit. One IQ does not a quality management system make.

However, some IQs send a strong signal that a company is serious about developing a quality management system. These signals come from companies that conduct regular Baldrige self-assessments, receive supplier awards from well-managed customers, or implement Six Sigma, EVA, and/or a Balanced Scorecard. While companies that do one or more of these things don't always end up making the well-managed category, they stand a much better chance of success than failure because of the systemic impact of these processes.

To show you what I mean, I did a quick search of SEC filings by two key words: Baldrige and EVA. I planned on searching for supplier award winners as well but didn't have to when I came across one during my Baldrige search.

My first example described in its 1994 annual report (published in early 1995) how it had implemented a self-assessment process using the Baldrige criteria. Olin Corporation (OLN) is a small-cap stock in the synthetics industry. Its experience from 1994 to 1998 reflects Honeywell's results with internal self-assessments. If you had invested in Olin when its annual report was published, your stock would have doubled in value in three years before tumbling in 1998 (Figure 8.7).

Computer Task Group (TSK) proudly announced in its 1995

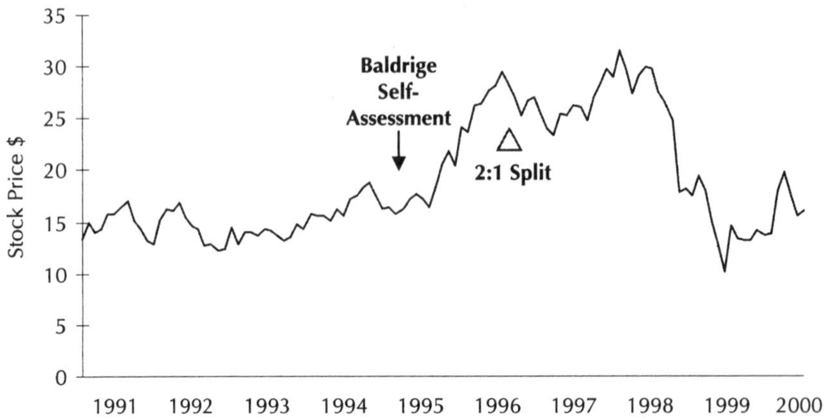

Figure 8.7 Olin Corporation's Stock Performance with IQ Milestone

annual report that it was the first IT supplier to receive the Distinguished Supplier Award from Baldrige Award-winner Milliken & Company. Like a Baldrige or state quality award, supplier awards are excellent independent validation of a company's management system. An investment in Computer Task Group based on that award would have earned strong returns until early 1998 (Figure 8.8).

You may be familiar with Equifax as one of the groups that provides credit reports. A holding company that also offers payment, cardholder and merchant processing, and other services, Equifax described its reliance on EVA in its 1994 annual report (issued in early 1995). An investor reading that annual report, taking the implementation of EVA as an early sign of an improving management system, and investing in Equifax would have tripled his or her investment in four years (Figure 8.9).

As you can see, I didn't trot out flawless performers for my examples. The stock of all three of these companies has suffered recently, affirming that no company, no matter how well-managed, exists in a

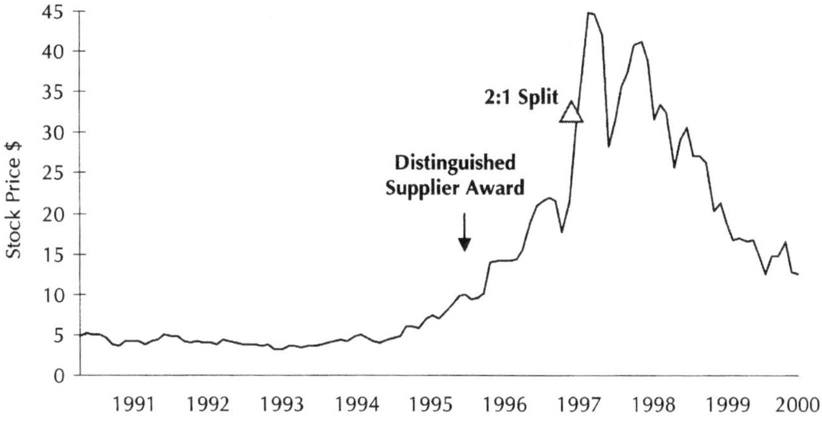

Figure 8.8 Computer Task Group's Stock Performance with IQ Milestone

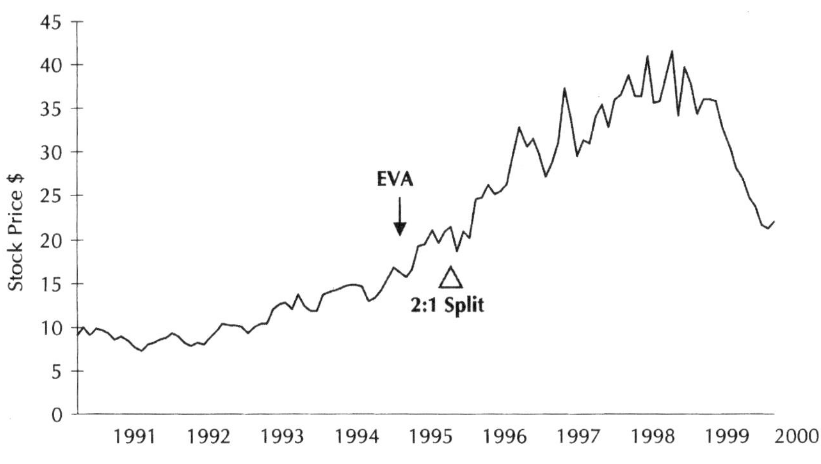

Figure 8.9 Equifax's Stock Performance with IQ Milestone

perfect world. In all three cases an investor would have enjoyed a nice return for two to four years, well beyond the length of time most investors hold onto a stock.

Before investing in a company based on one indicator of quality, you'll want to study its industry to identify financial trends and learn what qualifies as well-managed. You'll want to read up on industry trends and analysts' projections. You'll need to do key word searches to see if other IQs appear or if the company has been pursuing quality management longer than you first believed.

If the results of your research fail to tarnish your impression, just keep in mind the risk of investing in a company based on one indicator of quality, no matter how systemic it is.

When to Sell

In most cases, an investor will look to sell stock in a well-managed company when economic or industry factors threaten its value. Changes in microeconomic factors are much harder to track and, for that reason, less likely to trigger a decision to sell.

The most common stumbling blocks for a well-managed company are getting stuck on a performance plateau because the drive to improve runs out of steam, suffering bloat, or losing leadership.

You probably won't notice that a company has plateaued until its stock has plateaued as well. If that happens, run the Management Screen again to see if you get any recent hits that might tell you the company is still involved.

Well-managed companies have been known to suffer from bloated management systems built up during years of quality initiatives. About the only way to spot this from outside a company is by looking at revenue per employee compared with the industry average, or revenue per employee compared with previous years. If the company's performance is worse than either, it may be an indicator of growing bloat.

Losing leadership may be the most visible warning sign an investor has. In every well-managed company I know, the top person in the company has led the charge. When that person leaves, the relentless emphasis on quality management often leaves, too—not always, but often enough for investors to reconsider.

As the examples in this book show, scoring high on the Management Screen doesn't guarantee stellar stock performance. A company's management system is only one factor influencing its financial performance; stock in even the best-managed company cannot escape the punishment of rising interest rates, the fears of investors, or other external forces.

Yet despite its imperfections the Management Screen still gives investors an edge. As Robert Sheard wrote in *The Unemotional Investor* (Fireside, 1998), "the screen doesn't have to be perfect to be successful. All it has to be is better than average over long stretches of time and the investor using it will generate returns that would be the envy of professional money managers coast to coast."

The Q-100 proves the edge to be gained by investing in well-managed companies.

Chapter 9

Asset Plays and Factor Decay

When Federal Reserve Board Chairman Alan Greenspan appeared before the U.S. House Committee on Banking and Financial Services on February 17, 2000, he sought to explain the incredible productivity gains that drove the economy through the 1990s by laying the improvements at technology's doorstep. He pointed to "the synergies of the microprocessor, laser, fiber-optic glass, and satellite technologies" as technologies that "have dramatically decreased business operational uncertainties and risk premiums and, thereby, have engendered major cost reductions and productivity advances."

All this is true—to a point. What Mr. Greenspan misses, I believe, is what most economists, money managers, and other financial analysts miss, which is the impact on the economy of people working more efficiently. Technology certainly plays a big role in this, but only so far as a company's management system allows it. Well-managed companies take better advantage of new technologies but that is only one arrow in their quill. They also take better advantage of their people and processes, improving revenues while reducing costs to increase shareholder value.

All of this bodes well for American business. While the boost from technology will surely wane, the steady improvements in management systems will continue indefinitely, spurred by those few well-managed companies that continually raise the bar for everyone else.

As you've seen in this book, quality management is much more than having a reputation for quality products or services, just as it's much more than using new technologies wisely. That's a very narrow definition of quality limited to a small part of a company's management system. Well-managed companies see the whole. They work on the system. They build shareholder value through the synergies of visionary leadership, an uncompromising customer focus, empowered employees, and ever-improving processes.

The fact that not many companies have the knowledge or will to develop quality management systems gives those that do an edge, and that edge is reflected in the stock performance of well-managed companies.

That edge can take the form of a profitable investment for investors able and willing to screen for managerial competence. Quality of management becomes an *asset play* thanks to Wall Street's narrow view of what constitutes quality management. As long as the Street continues to overlook the value generated by well-managed companies, the asset play will continue to pay off.

Of course, there's always the chance that analysts and brokers will recognize a bargain and devote more attention to quality companies. There's also a chance that more companies will realize that improving the quality of their management systems makes good business sense. If that happens, some of the profits to be gained from well-managed companies will be arbitraged away because (1) more people will be investing in them and (2) more companies will qualify as well-managed, reducing the competitive advantage of managerial competence.

This erosion of value is called *factor decay*. When a quality management system's value as a predictor of above-average return on investment starts to diminish, factor decay has begun. I happen to think quality management will remain an asset play for a long time yet before factor decay sets in, but I also believe it's only a matter of time before Wall Street catches on.

It's already picked up the scent. A growing number of economists, analysts, and investors are wrestling with what's being called the New Paradigm, a rationale for America's strong economy that's based on strong productivity gains that are making companies more efficient.

I'd argue that they've got the New Paradigm backwards, that the strong economy has resulted from companies becoming more efficient which, in turn, has improved their productivity. Through that lens, quality is not only alive and well, it's playing a vital role in the productivity gains that have given us unparalleled growth without inflation.

We're at the beginning of an important dialogue about what quality management means to investors, business, and our economy. I invite you to weigh in with your opinions at www.baldrige.com, trade the names of well-managed companies, and help me improve the Management Screen.

I also encourage you to include the Management Screen in your investment decision-making process. At this point in time, you're in a great position to benefit from screening management quality because not many others are doing it.

Invest in the best and you, too, can profit from well-managed companies.

Appendix A

The Management Screen

To complete the Management Screen Evaluation Sheet at the end of this Appendix, assign points for each area below based on information you find about a company's management system. Guidelines for completing the screen can be found in Chapters 6 and 7. You may want to copy the Management Screen Evaluation Sheet for use with multiple companies; you can also download a copy of the evaluation sheet at www.baldrige.com.

1.0 Leadership
20 points possible: 12 points for 1.1 and 8 points for 1.2.

1.1 Senior leaders make quality management a top priority.

- Is the company guided by a single vision, focused on its customers, and promoting a work environment of empowerment and innovation?
- Do the president or chief executive officer (CEO) and other senior leaders talk about quality improvement's critical role in the company's success?
- Are senior leaders personally involved in quality improvement through such activities as conducting and taking training, recognizing exceptional performance, and encouraging learning and innovation?

1.2 The company and its people practice good citizenship.
- Is the company considered an ethical and responsible corporate citizen?
- Do the company and its employees actively support their communities?

2.0 Strategic Planning

20 points possible: 12 points for 2.1 and 8 points for 2.2.

2.1 The company has an effective strategic planning process.
- Does the company have a strategic planning process?
- Is there evidence the process involves a cross-section of employees, as is true with *Hoshin* planning, management by policy or planning, or strategy deployment?
- Does the company consider many types of information when constructing its plan, such as SWOT analysis, scenario planning, or customer and supplier input?

2.2 The company deploys its strategic plan throughout the organization.
- Is there evidence the company cascades its plan throughout the organization and aligns all activities with the plan?
- Does the company have key performance indicators (KPIs) or measures for tracking progress on its plan?

3.0 Customer and Market Focus

20 points possible: 16 points for 3.1 and 4 points for 3.2.

3.1 The company delivers products and/or services that satisfy customer requirements.
- Is there evidence of processes the company uses, such as customer advisory councils, market research, surveys, and/or Voice of the Customer, to understand what its customers require?
- Does the company have a formal process, such as Quality Function Deployment (QFD), for translating customer requirements into product and service designs?

- Does the company measure customer satisfaction on a regular basis (i.e., annually, quarterly, monthly, weekly)?
- Has the company received supplier awards from one or more customers?

3.2 The company builds and maintains strong customer relationships.

- Is there evidence the company has significant repeat business, a high rate of customer retention, and/or a high percentage (50% or above) of "very satisfied" customers?

4.0 Information and Analysis

20 points possible: 10 points for 4.1 and 10 points for 4.2.

4.1 The company has a performance measurement system.

- Does the company use a Balanced Scorecard or other formal measurement system that identifies and aligns key performance indicators (KPIs)?
- Does the company compare its performance to that of key benchmarks such as industry leaders and world-class companies?

4.2 The company analyzes performance measurements to assess its overall health.

- Does the company analyze different types of performance measurements through such tools as economic value-added and activity-based cost accounting?
- Does the company benchmark other companies to learn best practices and improve?

5.0 Human Resource Focus

20 points possible: 12 points for 5.1 and 8 points for 5.2.

5.1 The company promotes high performance by enabling employees to contribute effectively.

- Does the company promote flexibility, innovation, and knowledge sharing among employees through such means as teams and cross-training?

- Does the company invest time and resources in the training and education of its employees?
- Does the company recognize the contributions of its employees and reward them through such plans as profit sharing, gain-sharing, and Employee Stock Ownership Plans (ESOPs)?

5.2 The company has safe, motivated, and satisfied employees.

- Does the company publicly declare the value it places on its employees?
- Do employees express positive feelings about working for the company?

6.0 Process Management

20 points possible: 12 points for 6.1 and 8 points for 6.2.

6.1 The company systematically manages and improves its processes.

- Does the company display process thinking, as evidenced by process improvement teams, process innovation, reengineering, or other process improvements?
- Does the company use approaches such as Six Sigma, ISO 9000, QMS, or *Kaizen* to manage and improve its processes?
- Does the company include support functions such as finance, human resources, and sales in its process improvement activities?

6.2 The company systematically manages and improves its supplier interactions and processes.

- Does the company formally evaluate supplier performance through such methods as supplier scorecards or report cards?
- Does the company develop long-term supplier relationships through such activities as supplier certification, supplier partnerships, or supplier involvement on design teams and in strategic planning?

7.0 Business Results
80 points possible: 16 points each for 7.1, 7.2, 7.3, 7.4, and 7.5.

7.1 The company demonstrates measurable leadership in satisfying its customers.

- Does the company have data and information such as customer satisfaction survey results, supplier awards, customer retention rates, or independent ratings that demonstrate its customers' satisfaction?
- Does the company demonstrate customer satisfaction leadership compared to its competitors?

7.2 The company demonstrates measurable leadership in its financial performance.

- Does the company show improvement or have high performance levels in financial and market measures such as revenue, profits, cash-to-cash cycle time, earnings, market position, or market share?
- Does the company demonstrate financial and market leadership compared to its competitors?

7.3 The company demonstrates measurable leadership in employee satisfaction, development, and performance.

- Does the company have data and information such as safety, turnover, absenteeism, employee satisfaction, training hours per employee, or independent recognition that demonstrate employee satisfaction, development, and performance?
- Does the company demonstrate human resource leadership compared to its competitors?

7.4 The company demonstrates measurable leadership in the performance of its suppliers.

- Does the company have data and information such as supplier quality levels, number of certified suppliers, or reductions in waste, inventory, or cycle time that demonstrate supplier performance?
- Does the company demonstrate supplier quality leadership compared to its competitors?

7.5 The company demonstrates measurable leadership in organizational performance.

- Does the company have data and information such as cycle time reduction, quality improvement, cost savings, productivity improvement, or third-party assessments (ISO, QMS) that demonstrate organizational effectiveness?
- Does the company demonstrate organizational performance leadership compared to its competitors?

Management Screen Evaluation Sheet

Company: Date:

	Examples of Indicators of Quality (IQs)	*My Sources of Information*	*Statement Score*	*Category Score*
1.0 Leadership				
1.1 Senior leaders make quality management a top priority.	Executive communication			
1.2 The company and its people practice good citizenship.	Company foundations, community involvement, national recognition			
2.0 Strategic Planning				
2.1 The company has an effective strategic planning process.	Strategic plan, *Hoshin*, policy deployment, SWOT, scenario planning			
2.2 The company deploys its strategic planning process throughout the organization.	Plan alignment, KPIs			
3.0 Customer and Market Focus				
3.1 The company delivers products and/or services that satisfy customer requirements.	Customer advisory councils/ focus groups, Voice of the Customer, QFD, supplier awards			
3.2 The company builds and maintains strong customer relationships.	High retention rate, repeat business			

	Examples of Indicators of Quality (IQs)	*My Sources of Information*	*Statement Score*	*Category Score*
4.0 Information and Analysis				
4.1 The company has a performance measurement system.	Balanced Scorecard, KPIs			
4.2 The company analyzes performance measurements to assess its overall health.	EVA, ABC, benchmarking, Balanced Scorecard			
5.0 Human Resource Focus				
5.1 The company promotes high performance by enabling employees to contribute effectively.	Teams, cross-training, company university, ESOP, profit sharing			
5.2 The company has safe, motivated, and satisfied employees.	Best Company to Work For, family friendly, high employee satisfaction			
6.0 Process Management				
6.1 The company systematically manages and improves its processes.	Six Sigma, ISO, QS, *Kaizen*, reengineering, process improvement			
6.2 The company systematically manages and improves its supplier interactions and processes.	Supply chain management, supplier certification, supplier report cards			

	Examples of Indicators of Quality (IQs)	*My Sources of Information*	*Statement Score*	*Category Score*
7.0 Business Results				
7.1 The company demonstrates measurable leadership in satisfying its customers.	Supplier awards, independent ratings, ACSI ratings			
7.2 The company demonstrates measurable leadership in its financial performance.	Revenue, ROIC, market share			
7.3 The company demonstrates measurable leadership in employee satisfaction, development, and performance.	Training hours, turnover, employee satisfaction, independent recognition			
7.4 The company demonstrates measurable leadership in the performance of its suppliers.	Supplier certification			
7.5 The company demonstrates measurable leadership in organizational performance.	Six Sigma, ISO, QS, quality improvement, cycle time reductions			
		Total Points:		

Appendix B

IQs: Indicators of Quality at Well-Managed Companies

Leadership IQs

- Shared vision
- Flat organization
- Team-based
- Industry leader
- Alignment of plans/processes/people
- Training participation
- Measurements/strategic plan cascaded
- Six Sigma
- Baldrige Award/criteria
- State quality award participation
- Shingo Prize
- *Kaizen*
- Balanced Scorecard
- Policy deployment
- Quality Steering Committee
- Benchmarking
- Best practices
- Economic value-added (EVA)
- Learning organization

- (Company) University
- 360° feedback
- Personal quality goals/measures
- Team participation
- Frequent customer visits
- Participation in customer/supplier advisory councils
- Total quality environmental management (TQEM)
- Leading corporate citizen

Planning IQs

- SWOT
- Scenario planning
- *Hoshin* planning
- Strategy deployment
- Management by policy
- Management by planning
- Core competencies
- KPIs

Customer IQs

- Customer focus groups
- Customer advisory councils
- Customer roundtable meetings
- Voice of the Customer
- Quality Function Deployment
- Customers involved in product/service design
- Customer surveys
- Industry studies/comparisons
- Supplier awards
- Complaint management process
- Customer delight/loyalty/retention
- Percentage "very satisfied" customers

Measurement IQs

- Balanced Scorecard
- Key performance indicators (KPIs)
- Activity-based cost accounting
- Economic value-added (EVA)
- Benchmarking
- Best practices

Employee IQs

- High-performance work teams
- Self-directed work teams
- Cross-functional teams
- Process improvement teams
- Quality improvement teams
- Job rotation
- Job classification
- Open book management
- Employee development plans
- Career planning
- Cross-training
- Problem-solving process training
- Quality tools training
- Just-in-time training
- Profit sharing
- Gain-sharing
- Employee Stock Ownership Plan (ESOP)
- Employee satisfaction survey
- Employee Assistance Program (EAP)

Process IQs

- Reengineering
- Process innovation
- Process improvement
- Agile manufacturing
- Lean manufacturing
- Just-in-time (JIT)
- Enterprise resource planning (ERP)
- Six Sigma
- Black belts
- ISO
- QS
- Shingo Prize
- *Kaizen*

Supplier IQs

- Supply chain management
- Logistics management
- Supplier quality management (SQM)
- Enterprise resource planning (ERP)
- Commodity teams
- JIT/JIT II
- Supplier partnerships
- Supplier Scorecard
- Supplier report cards
- Supplier certification

Appendix C

Companies in the Q-100

In September 1998, Robinson Capital Management began tracking a quality index consisting of 100 of the Standard & Poor's 500 companies. They chose 100 companies for the quality index based on a proprietary process for scoring management system quality. They weighted their index in the same way as the S&P 500 and diversified the list to align it with the S&P's sectors. When Standard & Poor's revises its index to add and subtract companies, Robinson Capital Management adjusts its index accordingly.

As of September 30, 1999, the following companies made up the Q-100 (stock symbols in parentheses). An asterisk denotes companies that have changed names, merged with another company, or been removed from the S&P 500 since September 30, 1999.

Adobe Systems (ADBE)
Aetna Inc. (AET)
Air Products & Chemicals (APD)
Alcan Aluminum Ltd. (AL)
Alcoa, Inc. (AA)
*AlliedSignal, Inc. (now Honeywell)
American Express Company (AXP)
Amgen Inc. (AMGN)
Anheuser-Busch Companies, Inc. (BUD)

Apache Corp. (APA)
Armstrong World Industries (ACK)
Ashland Inc. (ASH)
AT&T Corporation (T)
Bank One Corporation (ONE)
Baxter International Inc. (BAX)
Bemis (BMS)
Bethlehem Steel (BS)
Black & Decker Corporation (BDK)
Boise Cascade Corporation (BCC)
Bristol-Myers Squibb Company (BMY)
Campbell Soup Company (CPB)
Carolina Power & Light Company (CPL)
Caterpillar, Inc. (CAT)
*CBS, Inc. (CBS)
Ceridian Corporation (CEN)
Chevron Corporation (CHV)
Cisco Systems, Inc. (CSCO)
Citigroup, Inc. (C)
Consolidated Edison (ED)
Constellation Energy (CEG)
Corning Incorporated (GLW)
Cummins Engine Company, Inc. (CUM)
Dell Computer Corporation (DELL)
Dominion Resources, Inc. (D)
Duke Energy Corporation (DUK)
I.E. duPont de Nemours and Company (DD)
Dun & Bradstreet (DNB)
Eastman Kodak Company (EK)
Emerson Electric Company (EMR)
Enron (ENE)
*Exxon Corp. (XON)
FDX Corporation (FDX)
Fluor Corp. (FLR)
Ford Motor Company (F)
FPL Group (FPL)

Gannett Inc. (GCI)
General Electric Company (GE)
General Motors (GM)
Gillette Co. (G)
GTE Corporation (GTE)
Halliburton Company (HAL)
Hershey Foods (HSY)
Hewlett-Packard Company (HWP)
Ingersoll Rand (IR)
Intel Corporation (INTC)
International Business Machines Corporation (IBM)
International Paper (IP)
J.C. Penney Inc. (JCP)
Johnson & Johnson (JNJ)
JP Morgan & Company (JPM)
Lockheed Martin (LMT)
Loews Corporation (LTR)
Lucent Technologies, Inc. (LU)
Marriott International, Inc. (MAR)
MBNA Corporation (KRB)
Medtronic, Inc. (MDT)
Merck & Company, Inc. (MRK)
Merrill Lynch & Company, Inc. (MER)
Microsoft Corporation (MSFT)
Minnesota Mining and Manufacturing Company (MMM)
*Mobil Corporation (MOB)
Morgan Stanley Dean Witter (MWD)
Motorola, Inc. (MOT)
Nike Inc. (NKE)
Nordstrom, Inc. (JWN)
Northern Trust (NTRS)
Parker Hannifin (PH)
Philip Morris (MO)
Procter & Gamble Company (PG)
Quaker Oats Company (OAT)
Rockwell International (ROK)

Sears, Roebuck and Company (S)
Snap-On Inc. (SNA)
Solectron Corporation (SLR)
Southern Company (SO)
St. Paul Companies, Inc. (SPC)
Staples Inc. (SPLS)
SuperValu, Inc. (SVU)
Tandy Corporation (TAN)
Texas Instruments, Inc. (TXN)
Timken Company (TKR)
Union Carbide (UK)
Union Pacific Corporation (UNP)
Unisys (UIS)
Unum Provident (UNM)
Wal-Mart Stores (WMT)
Walt Disney Company (DIS)
Wells Fargo (WFC)
Weyerhaeuser Company (WY)
Whirlpool Corporation (WHR)

Appendix D

Profile of a Well-Managed Company: Solectron Corporation

The following profile illustrates how excellence in many areas contributes to a quality management system. The profile gives you a measuring stick you can apply to companies under consideration as possible investments. Few, if any, will exhibit Solectron's managerial competence, but if they are serious about becoming more competent, they will be addressing the same elements of a quality management system highlighted in this profile.

Throughout the profile I've highlighted Indicators of Quality (IQs) and noted where they fit in the Management Screen (Appendix A). You'll notice systematic processes or world-class results for six of the seven Baldrige categories. The only category I didn't highlight was Information and Analysis; however, the presence of measures and analysis is apparent in every part of this profile.

Malcolm Baldrige National Quality Award 1997 Winner—Solectron Corporation

Through a deepening and broadening commitment to quality and performance excellence, Solectron Corporation, an electronics design and manufacturing services firm headquartered in Milpitas, California, has doubled its market share since 1992 and achieved a compound annual sales growth rate of 47% (Management Screen 7.2). Careful execution of this commitment on a global scale also has earned the rapidly expanding company its second Baldrige Award.

Solectron has sustained its rapid growth with something new—12 additional production and design facilities—and something old—satisfied repeat customers who have greatly increased their outsourcing business with the contract supplier. Contract spending levels by Solectron's 11 key, long-term customers increased 600% between 1992 and 1996, a solid indication of high levels of customer loyalty and satisfaction (7.1).

To maintain its corporatewide emphasis on quality as it expands globally, the company has designed a "new site startup process" based on the Baldrige Award criteria, helping to ensure that the new facilities are aligned tightly with regional customers' requirements and expectations (6.1).

The Business

Solectron Corporation is a worldwide provider of electronics design, manufacturing, and support services to leading original equipment manufacturers. It offers a broad range of premanufacturing, manufacturing, and postmanufacturing solutions. It also oversees materials logistics, managing customers' supply chains to meet product schedules.

Founded in 1977, Solectron is a publicly held company with revenues of $3.7 billion in fiscal year 1997. Dr. Ko Nishimura is chairman, president, and chief executive officer of the company, which employs more than 18,000 employees at 17 sites around the world.

Pursuing Excellence

Solectron aims to provide its outsourcing customers with significant competitive advantages: access to advanced manufacturing technologies, shortened time-to-market, reduced cost of production, and more effective use of assets. To do this, it must be intimately familiar not only with customers' immediate needs but also with their long-term product and market plans (3.1).

Effectively responding to today's and tomorrow's requirements is the goal of Solectron's three-pronged planning process. It encompasses an annually updated three-year strategic plan, an annual operating plan, and an annual improvement plan that sets, among other goals, stretch targets for all units and processes within the company (2.1).

Annual corporate business goals and improvement targets are set by Nishimura. At the same time, regional executives and the general managers at each production site determine their targets on the basis of their knowledge of customer requirements. Another round of planning aligns corporate goals with regional and site targets, while the company's global account managers ensure that the requirements of customers served by several Solectron facilities will be met.

The result is an "entrepreneurial" annual operating plan. Individual plans for each account and each site support Solectron's strategic objectives for building markets and strengthening capabilities. Yet, managers have considerable freedom in determining how best to achieve goals for financial performance, customer satisfaction, and employee satisfaction (2.2).

Opportunities for improvement are identified through the Solectron Total Quality Excellence Award Program, an internal version of the Baldrige Award assessment process (6.1).

Customer Focus

For over 10 years, Solectron has tracked customer satisfaction on a weekly basis, with an 80 to 90% survey response rate. Scores for delivery, quality, and service are at or nearing the 90% satisfaction level. This level of satisfaction is particularly noteworthy given the company's stringent rating scale in which a "C" receives a score of 0 and a "D" receives a score of minus 100. Grades of "B–" or lower trigger

Solectron's Customer Complaint Resolution Process. Within 24 hours, the account's program manager contacts the customer to acknowledge the issue and to gain additional information, and within 72 hours, a corrective action plan is submitted to the customer (3.1).

Customer-satisfaction report cards are reviewed weekly by managers and employees at each site. Nishimura reviews composite scores at each site during his quarterly visit (3.1).

Through an annual, third-party survey of executives at customer companies, Solectron again evaluates satisfaction levels and gathers information on customers' future business plans and manufacturing requirements. Respondents also are asked to rate Solectron relative to its competitors in the areas of quality, delivery, service, technical capability, material management, and overall satisfaction (3.1).

Survey results point the way to improvements in manufacturing and service capabilities that Solectron must make to meet future expectations and build new business. An example of customer-driven improvements is the newly added capability for automating exchange of customers' computer-aided designs. The technology has reduced the startup time for new projects by a factor of five. Another is greater emphasis on EDI (electronic data interchange) to link suppliers and improve on-time delivery rates. Use of EDI has yielded savings ranging between $25 and $260 per transaction (7.5).

Supply Chain Management

Solectron's purchases of materials and other items from suppliers total more than $2 billion annually—over 75% of company revenues. A key goal is to create value through supply chain design and management. The company issues quarterly report cards to preferred suppliers, marking them on key performance and price measures and issuing a "total cost of ownership" score (6.2).

Encouraging Employees

Solectron aims to create a work environment in which individuals can maximize their potential "by working both hard and smart, and doing what it takes to satisfy the customer."

Solectron University, established in 1990, drives management and employee skill development, supporting Solectron's philosophy to "hire for traits—train for skills" (5.1).

The company's variable compensation plan extends to all members of the workforce. Employee payout is based on individual, team, site, and corporate performance in the areas of revenue, profit, customer satisfaction, and operational performance (5.1).

Results

Solectron's commitment to manufacturing quality products and its strong performance management are reflected in key measures of financial performance, such as revenue growth and earnings per share. Since 1991, revenue growth has averaged well above the company goal of 25% annually and the electronics manufacturing services industry's average annual growth rate of 10%. As a result, Solectron's market share has doubled since 1992. In addition, over the past six years, Solectron's stock performance has significantly outpaced its largest competitor and the S&P 500, increasing sixty-fold since its initial public offering in 1989 (7.2).

Social responsibility is a foundation for improvement efforts. The company has reduced hazardous wastes and chemical emissions and now recycles 94% of materials. Because of its proactive approach, Solectron facilities in California, Texas, France, and Malaysia received local awards and recognition for environmental responsibility (7.5). In addition, the company has received more than 140 recognition awards from its customers since 1981 (7.1).

Appendix E

Resources

Invest in the Best Web Site (www.baldrige.com)

For links to sites identified in this book and new sites added since the book was published, visit www.baldrige.com. The site provides a downloadable copy of the Management Screen Evaluation Sheet and an updated graph showing the Q-100's most recent performance.

To get in touch with the author:

Stephen George
3381 Gorham Ave., Ste. 203
Minneapolis, MN 55426
(952) 927-7437
E-mail: SteveGeorge@baldrige.com

Robinson Capital Management

Robinson Capital Management created the Q-100. Feel free to contact Craig Robinson at:

Robinson Capital Management
5100 Eden Ave.
Edina, MN 55436
(952) 927-6799

Baldrige National Quality Program

The Baldrige Award program is a public/private effort managed by the National Institute of Standards and Technology. You can find out more about the Baldrige Award criteria, winners, and conferences at www.quality.nist.gov. The site also offers information about becoming a Baldrige examiner, which is a great way to learn what well-managed really means.

U.S. Department of Commerce, Technology Administration
National Institute of Standards and Technology
Baldrige National Quality Program
Administration Building, Room A635
100 Bureau Drive, Stop 1020
Gaithersburg, MD 20899-1020

Index